D0455428

I've Got Your Back

I've Got Your Back

Coaching Top Performers from
Center Court to the Corner Office

Brad Gilbert with James Kaplan

Portfolio

PORTFOLIO

Published by the Penguin Group

Penguin Group (USA) Inc., 375 Hudson Street, New York, New York 10014, U.S.A.

Penguin Group (Canada), 10 Alcorn Avenue, Toronto, Ontario, Canada M4V 3B2 (a division of Pearson Penguin Canada Inc.)

Penguin Books Ltd, 80 Strand, London WC2R 0RL, England

Penguin Ireland, 25 St Stephen's Green, Dublin 2, Ireland (a division of Penguin Books Ltd)

Penguin Group (Australia), 250 Camberwell Road, Camberwell, Victoria 3124, Australia (a division of Pearson Australia Group Pty Ltd)

Penguin Books India Pvt Ltd, 11 Community Centre, Panchsheel Park, New Delhi – 110 017, India

Penguin Group (NZ), Cnr Airborne and Rosedale Roads, Albany, Auckland 1310, New Zealand (a division of Pearson New Zealand Ltd)

Penguin Books (South Africa) (Pty) Ltd, 24 Sturdee Avenue, Rosebank, Johannesburg 2196, South Africa

Penguin Books Ltd, Registered Offices: 80 Strand, London WC2R 0RL, England

First published in 2004 by Portfolio, a member of Penguin Group (USA) Inc.

10 9 8 7 6 5 4 3 2 1

LIBRARY OF CONGRESS CATALOGING-IN-PUBLICATION DATA
Gilbert, Brad.
I've got your back : coaching top performers from center court to the corner office / Brad Gilbert with James Kaplan.
    p. cm.
ISBN 1-59184-047-3
1. Tennis—Coaching. 2. Tennis—Psychological aspects. 3. Tennis—Conduct of life. I. Kaplan, James. II. Title.
GV1002.9.C63G55 2004
796.342'07'7—dc22   2004040104

This book is printed on acid-free paper. ∞

Printed in the United States of America

To Chiv, for setting a standard of excellence
To A.A., for his vision to give me my first coaching job
To Andy, for his youth and exuberance
For Kimmie, because she's always "got my back"
To Zack, Jules, and Zoe, because they've got my heart

Forewords

Brad Gilbert's amazing eight-year run with Andre Agassi gave him quite a reputation on the pro tennis tour: He was the genius coach of all coaches. So when I started to work with him in mid-2003, I was as intrigued as anybody else in our world might have been: What complicated winning formula was Brad going to reveal to me?

The first big surprise was that there was nothing complicated at all.

"You've got a great game," he told me. "Now we're just going to take it down to your opponents' weaknesses."

What I discovered right away was that Brad's real genius was in making my life on the pro tour as simple as possible (which, of course, is a lot more complex than it sounds). For one thing, he has very few peers as a scout. He's brilliant at never taking anything for granted. Just because a guy was placing his second serve one way last week doesn't mean he's going to be putting it in the same spots this week. Things change every day on the tour, and Brad doesn't miss a single detail. He has an amazing pair of eyes, and they're always wide open.

He's also a master of what I call situational coaching: If I do *X* with the ball at a given point in a match, then my opponent's going to do *Y*. And if he's under pressure, he'll do *Z*. Still, I think Brad wants to show that there's a lot more to coaching than *X*s and *O*s. As skillful as he is at observing tennis, he's just as skillful at taking the pressure off.

I think we were both pleasantly surprised at the start of our working relationship to find out how much we had in common. We're both insane sports fans, both very outgoing and opinionated. It made what could've been an initially stressful situation easy and fun. And since Brad's natural style is to want to have fun, our good start just got better and better. Even our age difference became grist for the mill. Brad ragged on me for being a young punk, for wearing a visor; I ragged on him for being an old man, for not knowing who Maroon 5 is, for walking funny.

So much more goes into a player-coach relationship than just strategy. We eat together, we hang out, we have a blast. I kill him in Ping-Pong. I make him jump out of airplanes. (See Chapter 5!)

So when the moment comes that we have serious business to do, I not only feel completely comfortable; I completely believe in what Brad tells me. That's genius coaching—simple and complicated at the same time.

—Andy Roddick
May 2004

In early 1994, my ranking had fallen into the twenties, and I knew I wasn't playing as well as I could. I was looking for a new dimension in my game. Because I've always believed in surrounding myself with excellence, I began interviewing coaches, looking for the best there was. Brad Gilbert was the second person I talked to, and it quickly became clear that he was the right guy for me.

Brad was a friend from the pro tour, and we met over a pleasant dinner in Florida. He was all business that night. He broke my game down very efficiently; he told me things nobody else had. He said he thought I was depending too much on a take-no-prisoners style of play, one that required me to win every point, as opposed to getting my opponent to panic and lose the point. He felt I needed to think more on the court, to concentrate more on shot selection. He wanted me to become more of a percentage player.

Brad told me he felt I could be number three in the world. As soon as I told him he had the job, I made it my business to prove him wrong.

I'm going to call it like it is: In tennis, we have what you call *motivational coaches*—and to his credit, B.G. has never relied on being one of those. He's always believed in what he calls meat and potatoes. *X*s and *O*s. Brad firmly believes that the more prepared you are, the more positive you're going to feel. And he thinks that the best motivation of all is winning—getting to a point where what you're doing is just a lot of fun to do because you're doing it better than anybody else.

At the same time, he has always exuded tremendous positive energy for one fundamental reason: his deep and authentic love for the game. Brad is the kind of person who, when he cares about something, he cares about it with blinders—it's his life, his focus. That's the way he feels about the sport of tennis. He loves challenge, and he loves overcoming adversity.

For B.G., there was never a shortcut to success. When you stepped onto the court, you had to believe in yourself, based on your homework and preparation. What Brad helped me with the most was the ability to believe in myself by learning to think for myself. A great coach can lead you to a place where you don't need him anymore.

Brad Gilbert is a great coach.

—Andre Agassi
May 2004

Acknowledgments

My favorite tennis partners: Karen, Jacob, Aaron, and Avery
   My incomparable agent, Joy Harris
   My invaluable editor, Adrian Zackheim
   The indispensable David Bagliebter
   My tennis guru, Andrew Franklin
   And Brad Gilbert, who made it all easy and fun, and
opened up new dimensions of the game to me—and Brad's
wonderful family, who opened up their home to me.

—JK

Introduction   by Joe Kernen

On the face of it, you'd be hard pressed to think of two guys more different than Brad Gilbert and me. I talk about stocks on CNBC; Brad flies around the world coaching Andy Roddick. But the first thing you need to know about Mr. Gilbert is that he is a man of many parts, and an important side of him is that he's a dedicated investor in the stock market. Which is what—indirectly—led to our first meeting.

Back in the fall of 1997, when Brad was still coaching Andre Agassi, Andre hit a bit of a rough patch in his game. So rough was this patch that his ranking fell to an unbelievable 141 in the world. Andre wasn't too worried, though. He had his genius for tennis, and he had Brad. So when Cliff Drysdale interviewed Andre after a tournament and asked him if his ranking was going to return to its former heights, Andre looked into the camera and smiled that smile of his. "Like Joe Kernen would say, if I were a stock, you should buy me," Andre said.

Now, to this day I don't know whether Andre Agassi was

a dedicated viewer of my show or Brad Gilbert somehow put him up to making that remark, but I was pretty tickled, let me tell you. Soon afterward, I went out to dinner with Andre, at Campagnola, on Manhattan's Upper East Side. Halfway through the meal, in walked Brad Gilbert along with his wife, Kim. They make a pretty nice entrance, Brad and Kim. Kim is a tall, very pretty blond lady, and while I don't think anyone would call Brad pretty, he does have a certain athletic presence. Of course they spotted our table instantly. Brad saw me and smiled. "Hey, Super Joe!" he called.

The beginning of a beautiful friendship.

From that first night, I liked Brad for his easygoing, slightly off-the-wall style, the way he had of hitting the nail on the head with whatever he said, even if the way he said it seemed sideways at first. He appeared shy, but you discovered in a minute that his convictions about everything—sports, politics, finance, food, human behavior—were strong and deeply held. His knowledge was deep on many fronts. His powerful positive energy and his quiet, humorous way of connecting when he talked with you made me understand why he was a great coach.

I've Got Your Back fills out the picture. Who knew that Brad was not just a great tennis mind, but in a very real way, an important management guru? This is a book that can and should be read two different ways: as a source of delight for tennis fans eager to learn how Brad helped two great players, Agassi and Roddick, achieve their potential and as a source of enlightenment for anyone who wants to help the people he or she works with reach *their* highest potential.

Like many important leaders, Brad started out—in his days as a top-ranked tennis professional—as a bit of a diva. But when he made the move to coaching, he quickly came to the knowledge held by the Level 5 Leaders in Jim Collins's *Good to Great*: that personal humility in the service of a greater cause (the success of the team) is the most effective style of all.

When Brad started working with Andre Agassi, he'd never coached before, and so maybe a certain amount of humility came easy in those early days. He started thinking hard about what his own college coach, Tom Chivington— "Chiv"—had done and how he had done it. What he realized right away was that Chiv had taught in the best way possible: by example.

Brad's coach was that rarest of creatures: a strong but humble man, a natural Level 5 leader. Chiv had a quiet voice, enormous positive conviction, and when he traveled with Brad on the pro tour, the simple desire to do whatever it took to make Brad comfortable and at ease with himself, to put him in the frame of mind to win. This meant everything from getting laundry done to booking practice courts to scouting opponents. Chiv worked hard and cheerfully because he loved his work. He never raised his voice. He was an inspiration, commanding respect by acting respectfully.

So Brad set about adapting his own personal style—not merely copying Chiv's. He emphasized his best points (enthusiasm, engagement, awareness) and toned down his emotionalism and negativity. He extended his amazing powers of tennis observation to life off the court, learning important lessons about courtesy and humility from Agassi. Coach and player's respect for each other grew throughout their relationship and past it.

Then Brad took the lessons he'd learned to his work with Andy Roddick, and the relationship flowered. Each continues to learn from the other—and I know Brad is touched, amused, and inspired by Andy's youthful enthusiasm. The flexibility to adapt to a new style was one of the foundations Brad brought along from his earlier work. You can see the results on the sports pages.

Many of the images we have of coaches are negative: They're tough; they yell; they humiliate. Brad Gilbert, who is strong without being callous, is a very different kind of coach. One of his biggest points of pride is his ability to *pay attention*—whether scouting opponents or listening to a player. I would humbly suggest that anyone who pays attention to the multiple lessons in this book will feel inspired and gain the power to become inspiring.

We're all coaches.

—Joe Kernen of CNBC's *Squawk Box*

Contents

I've Got Your Back

Prologue: Mr. Gilbert to Serve

*A winning strategy takes guts, determination,
and confidence that you can beat the other guy.
How did humility get into it?*

"Hey, boss. I got breakfast."

—*B.G.*

Midtown Manhattan, August of 2003, and I'm on my way to buy Andy Roddick breakfast. Andy's back at the hotel, sleeping in: He's got a big day of practice ahead out at Flushing Meadows. Though he's just days away from turning twenty-one, this is his fourth U.S. Open, and it isn't overstating the case to say that the eyes of the tennis world are upon him. Since I started coaching him in June, at the Queen's tournament in London, Andy has gone on a blistering run, winning twenty-seven hard-court matches against one loss, and taking three hard-court titles in July and August, at Indianapolis, Montreal, and Cincinnati. He's number 4 in the world going into the Open. Suddenly he can't walk three steps without someone shoving a microphone in his face and asking if he's the Future of American Tennis. No pressure! My job is not just to prepare him for the tournament but to keep him on an even keel. Which means making him as comfortable as possible. Which, at this moment, means buying him breakfast.

There's a little deli on the East Side that makes bacon and eggs on a bagel just the way he likes it. A lot of people like the way these guys make breakfast—there's a line behind the counter that begins as soon as you walk in the door. I wait my turn. I'm wearing my Reebok warm-ups against the slight chill of the morning; my trademark black shades are propped up on top of my head. I've just turned forty-two years old, and there are a couple of strands of gray in my wiry black hair. I haven't shaved yet this morning, so I'm even woollier than normal.

My turn comes up, and one of the guys behind the counter nods to me. He recognizes me from yesterday morning. It doesn't matter to him that I used to be the number-4 tennis player in the world, or that I'm coaching the hottest kid on the pro tour. What matters to him is that I want two bagels, one with bacon and eggs, one with plain scrambled. To him I'm just a middle-aged guy in tennis clothes ordering breakfast.

That's fine with me. I enjoy the piece of fame I have in the tennis world; outside of that world I get recognized a little bit, but not a lot. I like people, I like to talk, and I don't need for someone to be in awe of me to have a good conversation. The counter man hands me my bag. I pay for the food, leave a couple of bucks in the tip cup, and head up the block to Starbucks. Andy wants an iced caramel macchiato to go with his bagel.

After I score the coffee, I flip out my cell phone and

call up to his room. "Hey, boss, I got breakfast," I say. "You ready? Excellent. I'll be up in a minute. See you, dude."

Now, I know what a few of you are thinking. Here's Brad Gilbert, made a few bucks over thirteen and a half years on the pro tour. Had a pretty good record against people like Jimmy Connors, Boris Becker, Andre Agassi, Michael Chang, and Pete Sampras. Coached Agassi for eight years, to five Grand Slam titles and a thirty-week number-1 run in 1995. *What is he doing going out to buy breakfast for a 21-year-old kid?*

And what am I doing calling a kid young enough to be my son boss? Have I fallen on hard times?

The answer to that last question is no. And as for the first two, I'll give you the beginning of an answer by filling in one bit of description I left out earlier. As I'm walking around Midtown Manhattan getting Andy Roddick his bagel and coffee, I'm smiling. I couldn't be happier. I love my job, and I want to tell you why.

Enthusiasm can't be faked. It must be found.

1. Tennis Lessons, Life Lessons

A coach shouldn't be just a boss, or a teacher, but a protector.

"John Wooden had so much love for talking about the team, and the foundation of the team, that he would never discuss a single player. He inspired every one of his players to put aside his ego in pursuit of excellence. How did he do it? By putting aside his own ego first."

—*B.G.*

ome people call me a great coach. After all, they say, I've taken two tennis players—one of them, Andre Agassi, slightly stuck in neutral and not playing the way he should; the other, Andy Roddick, a hot-tempered kid with genius but less than great discipline—to the very pinnacle of the game, at the very point when the world was starting to think about counting them out. There must be a magic wand in my tennis bag!

There is no wand. To those who call me great, I say thanks for the compliment, which I respectfully decline.

This isn't fake modesty. I love what I do, and I think I'm very good at it. But I am by no means infallible. And if I have any special skill—besides knowing as much as almost anybody out there about what goes on inside the 27 by 78 feet of a tennis court—it's that I'm pretty darn good at *paying attention*. And I've had the amazing fortune to have had at least two great teachers in my life to pay attention to.

One of them is named Andre Agassi.

What's this? Isn't the player supposed to learn from the coach, rather than the other way around?

Well, sure—sometimes. But show me a coach (or a boss) who doesn't listen—really listen—and I'll show you a probable loser. Show me a coach (or a boss) who domineers and demeans, who manages through fear, and I'll show you an accident waiting to happen. Show me a coach or a boss who doesn't think it's just as important to empower the lowliest scrub on the team as it is to cater to the star, and I'll show you a real short timer.

A true story, about a coach who's become an inspiration to me, Dick Vermeil, of the Kansas City Chiefs: Last summer, Dick gave a barbecue at his house for the entire team, not just the stars. Dick did all the cooking and every bit of the cleaning up, all by himself. No caterers, no maids, no hired help. And he was happy to do it. How do you think the Chiefs' third-string defensive tackle felt after that barbecue?

Like he was ready to move heaven and earth for Dick Vermeil, that's how.

Likewise, going to get Andy Roddick his morning coffee and egg sandwich when we're traveling together is one of my favorite things in life. It makes Andy feel totally taken care of; it makes me feel like a powerful guardian. It makes us feel like a team.

In fact, you might say I'm a team player in an individual sport. One of my coaching idols is UCLA's great former basketball coach, John Wooden. The man is ninety-three years old now, but he's still an inspiration. I saw Jamal Wilkes interviewed on TV a little while ago—here was a guy in his fifties, his face full of joy as he talked about his coach. (That's what he still calls him.) The interviewer asked Jamal if he still finds himself doing things in life that Coach Wooden taught him, and Jamal just beamed. "Every day," he said.

John Wooden has so much love for talking about the team, and the foundation of the team, that he will never discuss a single player. He inspired every one of his players to put aside his ego in pursuit of excellence. How did he do it? By putting aside his own ego first.

An expression I've used with both Andre and Andy is, "I've got your back." That says it all about me, in a nutshell. *I've got your back.* If it was four in the morning, and my guy called me up and said, "I need you to come over," I wouldn't ask what it was about. I wouldn't think twice. I would think once, and this is what my thought would be: *If it's important enough for him to call on me at that hour, it's important enough for me to go.* And whatever the situation was, we would figure it out. That's just the way I am. Or, I should say, the way I learned to be.

It all started with Chiv—Tom Chivington, the tennis coach of Foothill College in Los Altos Hills, California. Foothill is a community college, a two-year institution, a stop along the way for kids who, for whatever reason—emotional, financial, academic—need a little boost before they can make it in a four-year school.

I was a bit different. True, I was never much of a student (to put it mildly): Graduating from college wasn't my dream. No, I had this nutty idea that I could become a professional tennis player.

How nutty? In 1979 I was the number 35 junior player in the country. Which sounds pretty good—until you realize that at most only six or seven of the top ten juniors ever make it to the pros. I was a scrawny little runt who'd done amazingly well for a guy who didn't have much of a serve, volley, or backhand. My success, such as it was, was pretty much based on the fact that I was, first of all, fast on my feet and second, one tough little scrapper. It didn't matter if the other guy was bigger, stronger, better—I just kept coming. Never gave up. Took no prisoners. You'd be surprised how many matches that'll win you.

I was originally recruited to Arizona State, a good tennis school, but as soon as I reported to Tempe that fall, the coach who'd signed me got fired. The new coach brought in his own players, and I was told I could take a backseat. I decided to relocate. Foothill was close to my home in Piedmont, California, and for a junior college, it had a very strong tennis reputation, thanks to its coach, Tom Chivington.

On January 2, 1980, I reported to Foothill, their hot new singles prospect—and a definite question mark, in the coach's eyes. I was five foot eight, 120 pounds soaking wet, with big hair and a big attitude. (Little did I know that one day a kid named Andy Roddick—a kid who wasn't to be born for two more years—would give me a very hard time about that big hair.) Chiv, who talked softly but looked you right in the eye, put me on the spot. He'd heard I was a bit of a bad actor on the court.

I saw right away that this was a man I had to be straight with. I swallowed. "I've stepped over the bounds a few times," I admitted.

"Can we work on that?" Chiv asked me.

I didn't have to think twice. "That's what I'm here for," I told him.

It was the right answer. That day, for some reason, Chiv saw I was a work in progress and decided to take me on as a project. He knew I didn't have much game, but I almost made up for it with my fighting spirit. He resolved then and there to make a player out of me.

I told you I had mediocre strokes—the truth is that one of my shots was even worse than that. My backhand was strictly a defensive shot, pushed rather than struck, and I couldn't get out of jail with it. Any guy with a strong serve could spin it to my left side, cruise in to net, and have me for lunch.

Lots of coaches had tried to get me to change, but they

were always totally negative about it. "You have to do it like this or you're never going to be any good," they'd tell me. Or, "If you don't go to a two-handed backhand, you have no hope. Your backhand sucks. Your grip is terrible." It was always, "You can't, you won't." And my first thought was always, "How good were *you?*" That was my brashness talking. But I couldn't help it—it's always really ticked me off when someone tells me I can't do something. For a long time, my anger drove me more than anything else.

I could tell right away that Chiv was different. He was quiet and friendly—he had an incredibly calm voice—but he was firm at the same time. I knew he liked me, yet he also wasn't about to put up with any crap from me. When I showed up twenty minutes late to my very first tennis practice, he said, "That's the last time you will ever show up late—ever." I was genuinely puzzled: Nobody had ever called me on that before. But Chiv said, "If you don't come on time, you do not respect me." I was never late— for anything—again. In fact, I'm notorious for showing up a half hour early for everything.

I respected Chiv because he clearly knew what he was talking about, because he radiated self-respect and quiet authority, and because every day, at every practice, he was pumped just to be there—excited about working with every guy on the team, from the strongest to the weakest. I knew right away it was for real: That's the kind of thing you just can't fake. Chiv had been at Foothill his entire career, since the school opened its doors in the mid-sixties. He could have gone to many other schools, because he was a great coach, but he ended up just loving Foothill and creating a great tennis program there. His love for his job and the school were more important to him than personal prestige. That attitude was infectious. Some people would show up and act like, "Shit, I'm at a junior college." The first day I got there and met Chiv, I knew I was in the right place.

Positiveness was something that had been missing from my tennis career up to that point. I was tough, I was determined—but I was negative. Junior tennis had felt like a grind to me. I loved the game, but I hated the dog eat dog.

Chiv's spirit was contagious, and I caught it. I wanted to work hard and do well; I wanted to please him. I had always lived for competition, but now I began to love it.

The next lesson took a little longer. A positive fighting spirit was all well and good, but I needed a backhand to go with it. Chiv had a friend with a private court, and on weekends he and I would go over there with a basket of balls, and he'd feed me five hundred backhands. The goal was to try and turn my defensive chip into an offensive topspin shot without changing my funky continental grip. It ain't easy—try it sometime.

But after two months, I figured it out: Suddenly I could hit over my backhand with confidence. And miraculously, something else happened at the same time. I grew. Five inches and five pounds in eight weeks. All at once, I was a six-foot-one-inch, 125-pound beanpole.

The weight would come, but now that I had the height—and the stroke—I started to turn the tables on the competition. Suddenly, guys who had been regularly cleaning my clock, 6–2 and 6–1, were falling to me by the same scores. By the end of my freshman year I had gone from being a semi-crappy former junior to a player who was ready, I thought, to play on the pro tour. Except for one thing: I lost in the finals of the California state championships. "I think you need to show me you can at least be number 1 in California," Chiv said, "before you go on to the next level."

He was right, as usual. I corrected that situation the following year. Not only did I win the state championships, I didn't lose a single varsity match as a sophomore at Foothill. I also made the Junior Davis Cup team, the first junior-college player ever to do so. But Chiv had more to teach me. Even though I was the clear-cut number 1 on the Foothill team, head and shoulders above everybody, he made me defend my spot in challenge matches. He didn't want me getting above myself or complacent; he also didn't want anyone else on the team to feel that the coach was playing favorites. If I was going to be a star, I had to show it through my deeds, not my attitude.

I was hot to drop out after sophomore year and start

playing the pro tour. Chiv had a different idea. "You should go win the NCAA Championships," he told me. "It's just a waste of time," I told him. Chiv gave me a look. "You only have one shot in your life at trying to win the NCAA," he said. "And if you win, it could give you a big boost when you go out on the tour"—Nike and Adidas were giving out some pretty big contracts in those days to NCAA winners.

I saw his point.

In January of 1982, I transferred to Pepperdine University in Malibu in order to be eligible for the NCAA Championships. (My relationship with Chiv would have another chapter, even though I didn't know it at the time.) I stayed at Pepperdine exactly one semester, playing under the one-of-a-kind Allen Fox, a great tennis mind and a quirky character, who taught me a bit more about staying positive. I remember one time I was playing like crap in a match, down 5–2 in the third set. It had turned into the kind of match I call a trunk slammer: When you're all ready to throw your sticks in your gear bag, throw the bag in the trunk of your car, and get the hell out of there. Foxy came out onto the court, walking his goofy little duckwalk, looked at me, grinned, and said, "You got him right where you want him." I said, "Coach, what are you talking about? I'm down 5–2 in the third." "No problem," Foxy said. "He's so nervous about winning, you can take it from him, right here." It changed my whole mind-set about the match. Foxy always used to say, "You're never going to get three games back at once. Get one game back. Start with one game—then maybe you'll get two."

Often as not, it worked out just that way.

The NCAAs, though, were a different story. I had a great run in the tournament, then in the final I came up against Mike Leach, a huge-serving lefty from the University of Michigan. And I was guilty of two things: The first was arrogance. I simply *assumed* I was going to win that tournament. I had geared my entire game for the last half-year toward this moment; I had done everything right. In my mind, the title was mine already. The check was in the mail.

Mike Leach had a different plan.

The final score was 7–5, 6–3. In retrospect, I did several things wrong, including playing not to lose (always a big mistake) and not digging down when things got tight. I think maybe I got steamrolled mentally because I expected it to come a little easier. And because I was surprised at his game.

My worst mistake was not having the foggiest idea, before I walked out onto that court, what kind of tennis player Mike Leach was. I've heard it said that John McEnroe never scouted an opponent. Well, I've said it before and I'll say it again: Mac's a tennis genius. And it's nice to be a genius, but those of us who aren't have to work extra hard. For two weeks after that NCAA final, I walked around like I'd been kicked in the groin. Then I straightened up and came to my senses. Throughout my two years at Foothill and my short time at Pepperdine, I'd been pretty careful about at least watching my opponents warm up. This time, I hadn't been careful at all. Now I was on my way to the pros (with a small endorsement contract from Nike), where the competition would be much, much tougher. And I decided I was going to pay very, very close attention.

The tennis immortal Bill Tilden said, "Never change a winning game; always change a losing game." The great coach Tom Chivington said something just as important, in my opinion: "When do you change a losing game? When you have a better plan."

My first summer as a touring tennis pro, the summer of 1982, was rough. I was just one of hundreds of hungry young wannabes: Every one of us could play, every one of us desperately wanted a spot on the main tour. The only way to get there was to accumulate ATP points, and the only way to get those points was to play satellite tournaments and qualifiers. It was not glamour time. It was plane rides and bus rides, cheap motels (with three guys in a room) and fast food. It was bad practice courts or no practice courts. A lot of guys weren't up for the grind. They got homesick, they got injured, they dropped out.

But I was happy to be there. This was what I wanted to do with my life; I'd never imagined anything else. Even when it was 100 degrees and 200 percent humidity in Monroe, Louisiana, or Little Rock, Arkansas, or Sioux City, Iowa, I was thrilled to be out there battling, playing for a few dollars and a couple of points. I didn't win any of the tournaments on that satellite, but I came in fourth overall, which was good enough to get me into my first event on the main tour, the Washington Star International in Washington, D.C. I won my first round, a rough three-setter against Derek Tarr of South Africa, and lost in the second, to a Czech named Jiri Granat. I had picked up a few points and was now 190th in the world.

During my first year in the pros, I saw more and more of the up-and-comers come and go. It wasn't just home-sickness and injuries and the tough conditions at minor tournaments like Taipei that did them in; it was losing. Every tour hopeful had been hot stuff at some point in his life—in the juniors, in college. But once you started mixing it up with the world's best, you had to be ready to take some falls. It didn't feel good to lose, but you had to learn to shake it off and move on.

I was just good at that, I guess. I wasn't little anymore—I'd hit my fighting size of six one and 175 pounds—but I was still tough.

But tough ain't enough. You have to be smart, too. You

have to have a plan. If you lose to a guy, you can't exactly go punch him. You can't really do anything—except make sure you get a piece of him the next time you meet.

Well, there are two ways to accomplish that. One is to get better. But even improving your game won't take you the whole way. As I said in *Winning Ugly,* every victory in tennis is a combination of one player's strengths and the other player's weaknesses. And if you know the other guy's weaknesses, you have a huge leg up. Back when I was at Foothill, Chiv used to scout all my opponents for me. After my loss in the NCAA finals, I realized that maybe having had someone to do that for me had made me a little lazy. So when I started on the tour, I began keeping a little black book on every guy I played, and even on every guy I saw playing.

I guess a couple of things made me different from other up-and-comers on the tour. True, I had a positive attitude and resilience and foot speed. But other guys had those traits. What set me apart, maybe, was my eye for the game, my memory for how people played it (with the black book to back it up), and my drive to *pay attention.* Almost every other guy on the tour, when he was finished with his match, couldn't wait to get the hell out of there— to go back to the hotel room and watch TV, or go pound a few beers. Call me nutty (and a few people did), but I loved to hang out at the venue: watching matches or practice, shooting the breeze with guys in the locker room or training area. (I still love it.) And whenever I was watching tennis, I was taking notes—either in my memory, to write down later, or right into the little book.

There wasn't any rhyme or reason to my black book. If you'd ever seen it, you would not have been impressed. It was all just scribblings, but those chicken scratches meant a lot to me. I'd write a guy's name, and jot down three or four things about him: "Forehand—every time he gets tight, he misses it." Or, "Huge serve in the ad court; his money ball, that out-wide serve."

After a while, I had quite a few names in there, and quite a few pointed observations. And since the cast of characters on the tour was more or less constant, the odds were pretty good that, just from having watched a guy practice in Hartford, I already had a cool little scouting report on him when I had to face him in the third round in Hong Kong. Maybe I'd be in the bathroom before my match, reading about this guy's huge out-wide serve in the ad court. So I'd think, *Okay, I've got to take that away. Even if he hits a winner down the middle, I've got to stand in the alley to receive his big serve on the left side.* That book was the only coach I could afford in the early days, but it was worth its weight (and then some) in gold.

By the end of 1985, my ranking had climbed to 18 in the world. And since I was finally making some serious money,

I decided to marshal my forces for an assault on the top 10. What that meant was hiring a coach. I didn't have to think twice about who I wanted for the job.

Chiv had now been at Foothill for twenty years, and had made the school a real force in California collegiate tennis. His position of great respect (and a terrific assistant coach, in the person of Dixie Macias) allowed him to put together a deal with the school whereby he could travel with me during the fall quarter, from the U.S. Open till December. Once classes were out for the summer, he came on the road with me again. We worked together ten to fifteen weeks a year, for five years in a row: By 1990, largely thanks to Chiv, I reached my apex of number 4 in the world.

Chiv's one condition with me was that he be allowed to bring along his beloved wife, Georgie. Georgie coached the women's tennis team at Chabot College in Hayward, and she's really the female Chiv—she knows just about as much about the game as Tom does.

What did Chiv do for me? It had a lot less to do with my strokes and footwork (which were pretty sound by that point—they had to be!) than just making my life easy while I fought through the rigors of the tour. When you're on the road, it means a huge amount to have "little" things like food and laundry and practice-court time taken care of, so you can concentrate on tennis. Chiv would also carefully scout all my potential opponents, taking detailed notes on his ever-present clipboard. And he was an incredibly positive, nonjudgmental guy—the kind of guy who, since I tended to be a bit, shall we say, tightly wound, was very important for me to be around.

Chiv's levelheadedness meant a tremendous amount to me. There was never an angry word between us. No matter how badly I played, he never yelled at me once. (A lot of coaches, even in tennis, are of the Vince Lombardi/ Bobby Knight ream-'em-out-and-wake-'em-up persuasion.) And no matter how beautifully I won, unless it was a final, he never wanted either of us to get too excited. "Let's figure out what we're going to do tomorrow," Chiv would say.

Back to the meals and laundry for a second. At the time Chiv was in his mid-forties. And by now this must be ringing a bell for you: Wasn't there something strange about a middle-aged guy, a man of dignity and accomplishment, doing laundry and fetching breakfast for a guy in his mid-twenties?

My answer to that is: There are no menial jobs, only menial people. Chiv brought every ounce of his dignity and accomplishment to his work with me. And the main thing is, he loved the work. He loved me and believed in me. He was proud of his part in propelling me into professional tennis. And he was delighted to be able to do anything he could to help me achieve my potential. Back then, if I had called him at four in the morning with some problem, he wouldn't have asked any questions: He would've said, "I'll be right over." (I half suspect he still might.) He had my back.

His work made me feel totally taken care of; it made him feel like a powerful guardian. It made us feel like a team.

Neither of us knew it then, but Chiv was preparing me for my next step in life, a step I'd never dreamed of.

> Reassess your commitment to being a team player. No matter how good you are, you can do better.

Thanks to Tom Chivington—and, to give myself some credit, my own development as a human being—I learned a tremendous amount over the fourteen years between the day I first stepped onto the Foothill campus and 1994, the year that would be my last on the pro tour. I learned to love playing tennis, and to pay very close attention to every aspect of the game. I learned about something seemingly small but actually huge—the value of the clock.

There were a dozen other lessons, too, but one of them was so big that it took me a while to get my mind around it. I saw how Chiv's humility—putting Foothill's importance, and then my importance, before his own—had made him a great coach. I loved and appreciated every molecule of that man's being. *But that was Chiv,* I thought. I was Brad, a different guy altogether. Humility wasn't something for me: I needed my ego to power me through the very significant challenges of the men's professional tennis tour. When you're going up against ultraskilled, ultratough competitors every day of the week, being humble doesn't cut it.

That's the way it seemed to me at the time, anyway. Unbeknownst to me, however, I was about to acquire a new teacher.

2. Student Teaches

Chiv's work made me feel totally taken care of; it made him feel like a powerful guardian. It made us feel like a team.

"Never change a winning game, always change a losing game."

—*Bill Tilden*

"When do you change a losing game? When you have a better plan."

—*Tom Chivington*

T hank God for Andre Agassi. He knew I wanted to be a coach before I did. I didn't really know what I wanted to do. I certainly never planned to become the coach to two of the greatest players of our time. After all, I'd made a few million dollars in prize money during my playing career, and a few million more from endorsements. I could've hung it up and walked away—raised my family, managed my investments, and done all right.

But in March of 1994, my life turned one of those corners that life sometimes turns. I was playing at the Lipton Championships in Key Biscayne, Florida, just up the road from Miami. I was thirty-two years old, and I was still hitting a pretty decent ball, good enough to be ranked number 28 in the world. Then, one afternoon when I went out to warm up for my match, I ran into Andre on the practice court. We knew each other pretty well from the tour, and even though he was almost ten years younger than me, we were fairly close buddies. I liked the guy. A lot of the other players weren't crazy about his flamboyant style:

the wild hair (he used to have hair), the earrings. People thought he was cocky, aloof. To me, he was a guy who was warm and genuine—a kid who was in the process of becoming a man, under extremely challenging circumstances. I knew all about the pressures of the pro tour, and I felt for him. He had been nice to my young son and daughter at a tournament in Arizona a few weeks before, and I appreciated that. Plus, from the first moment I ever saw him play (at Stratton Mountain in 1986, at sixteen years old and around 120 pounds) I thought he was an awesome tennis talent.

But at that point early in 1994, he was a player at a crossroads. He was only twenty-three, but he'd already been on the pro tour for over seven years, and he'd gone places. He'd come on like a skyrocket in the late eighties and early nineties, winning his first ATP title at seventeen, reaching his first Grand Slam finals, at the French and U.S. Opens, in 1990, and winning Wimbledon (beating Becker and McEnroe in the process) in 1992. He'd risen as high as number 3 in the world, but he had gone down as low as the twenties. He had a reputation as a streaky underachiever—a potentially great player who wasn't living up to his potential. In particular, he'd managed to lose two French Open finals, in 1990 and 1991, against players he should have beaten.

When I caught up to him in Key Biscayne, he was coming back from wrist surgery, his ranking was down in the thirties, and unbeknownst to me, he was questioning himself a little bit. (Andre was seeded 24th in the tournament, I was 23rd.) I was pleased when he invited me out to dinner, at an Italian restaurant in a place called Fisher Island.

I'd never been to Fisher Island before. You drive your car onto a ferry to get there. The whole way, I kept feeling a little strange, as if I were crossing over to a new place in more ways than one.

Andre was already sitting on the deck of the restaurant when I got there; next to him sat his longtime best friend and manager/agent, Perry Rogers. We ordered our dinner out on the deck, and as the sun set and the boats cruised by in the channel, we drank a few beers. It was all very pleasant, except that after a couple of minutes, I realized I was in the middle of an interview for a job I had never even thought about doing.

Andre was asking me a million questions about the direction of his tennis game: What was he doing right these days? What was he doing wrong? Where should he be looking to go with it?

Now, I love to talk, and I especially love to talk about tennis. I believe I know a little something about the sport. And I had plenty of opinions about Andre's game, which I'd been watching closely since he started out. I thought his potential was limitless. I may have happened to be ranked higher than he was at the moment, but I knew enough about what I did for a living to realize that while I had talent, Andre hit a tennis ball the way God intended it to be hit.

Hitting the ball beautifully isn't enough, though. What stood out to me at that moment was that I sincerely believed Andre wasn't thinking enough about his game. In particular, he wasn't paying enough attention to his opponents' shortcomings. There wasn't a thing wrong with his strokes: He wasn't looking to me for technical improvement. What he needed was a strategist.

Maybe it was because I had a couple of beers in me, but the more I talked, the more excited I got. After an hour and a quarter, I said, "Andre, I really think I could help you become a great player."

"You think so?" he said.

I looked him in the eye. "Yes, I do," I said.

We began working together the next day: No trial period. No contract. Just a handshake. I made one change immediately. When we'd left the restaurant the night before, I said, "I'll get us a practice court at eleven A.M."

Andre gave me a look. He was notorious for being a night owl. "I never practice before two," he told me.

I smiled. "I'll see you at eleven," I said. "Don't be late."

I'm an early starter; Chiv was always an early starter. I believe in the beginning of the day. Your mind is clearer then. Things don't get a chance to fester if you start out early.

What's more, I wanted to establish discipline. Not dominance. After all, Andre was the boss—he could fire me if he wanted. But I wanted to forge a new kind of professional relationship.

At the same time, Andre and I were friends, and I wanted to make sure the friendship stayed alive. Some coaches need to keep the lines clear: When work is over, they go their separate ways. When Chris Mullin first started playing for Golden State, he'd say, "On our team, we have five guys, five cabs." To me, that sounded like the root of all evil. I knew I could never work with somebody unless we could hang out all the time: joke together, relax together, watch some ball on TV. Positiveness is all-important, and relaxation is a huge part of positiveness. Chris had so many coaches in the NBA who would scream at their players—they might've been right, but it didn't work. The message got lost.

Still, you can also be too meek. You have to be adaptable—watch your player carefully, work the angles. Be assertive sometimes, lay back other times. I can't say this often enough: *Every day is a different day.* Paying attention to the changes, and being flexible about them, can make or break a coaching relationship.

Even so, I needed to make clear to Andre that we were going to put nothing less than an all-out effort into our work together. If we were going to be in this thing together, we had to be a team. And a lot of the time, I'd have to be the one calling the shots.

A.A. had always been advised just to play his game—he could go right through most people that way. But beating most people doesn't take you to the top; it only gets you near the top. And especially now, when his ranking was down and his confidence wasn't all it could be, he had to be extracareful about hungry up-and-comers. It's a cliché that on the men's pro tennis tour, anybody, even number 450 in the world, can beat anybody else, even number 1, on a given day. It happens all the time.

But the last thing you want, especially if you're trying to climb back up the ladder, is to be on the wrong end of an upset. The best way to avoid it is not to leave anything to chance. I took out my little black book and went to work.

Andre's first opponent at Key Biscayne that year was a Brit named Mark Petchey. You've never heard of him; Andre had heard of him, but didn't know his game that well. But I did. I'd seen him play. He was around 100 in the world, and I knew Andre could beat him, but I also knew it wouldn't be a cakewalk, and I told him exactly why. I said, "All right, Andre. This guy is going to serve-and-volley on everything, and he's going to chip and charge when he has a chance." I gave him a ton of input. Andre couldn't believe how much I knew about Mark Petchey.

And it paid off. Andre ended up winning a very tough

three-setter against Petchey, a match made all the more difficult by the fact that Andre did not play well that day. We've all had it happen: You wake up on the wrong side of the bed, and nothing you do for the rest of the day feels exactly right. It's unpredictable, and it happens to the greats, too. And you have to be ready for it. It's easy to imagine the result of Agassi-Petchey having gone the other way—especially if Andre had known less about his opponent than he did. This is not to pat myself on the back. I was just doing the same thing for my guy that Chiv had done for me.

I thought I had absorbed every possible lesson from my coach. But as I would soon discover, I still had a lot to learn.

The pro tennis tour is a lonely grind, and a touring pro quickly learns one thing: Look Out for Number One. Self-absorption is a survival skill on the tour. If you start thinking about other people's feelings, you might start thinking about the feelings of the guy on the other side of the net from you—who, as I have noted elsewhere, is essentially out to take money from your kids' college funds. You're out there to win, not to be sensitive.

And the more you win, unfortunately, the less sensitive you're inclined to get. Successful tennis pros are showered with money and all kinds of other perks, along with so much conditional love from so many people that you quickly grow dependent on the coddling even as you feel suspicious of it. The result, for a player, is a very reasonable level of skepticism about people's motives, and an even deeper level of self-absorption.

None of this is exactly conducive to good manners. To my everlasting regret, I—like many other players—could be a bit of a jerk when I was on the tour. A lot of people who work behind the scenes at tournaments are volunteers, eager to be close to the action, excited to be around the stars. Most tournament workers aren't going to bat an eyelash when you tell (not ask) them to get you some practice balls or a few towels.

It dawns on me now, too—might as well get it all out— that I was also guilty of acting this way with Chiv. There were plenty of times, whether it was my morning coffee I wanted, or my laundry done, or my practice court booked, when I would simply say to him, "Can you do this for me?"— leaving out one very important word. Looking back, I wish I'd been more thankful in general. Because what I realize now is that both Chiv and Georgie did everything I asked so willingly. So gracefully. They weren't doing it for thanks, but because they loved it. They loved me. And they were devoted to a single goal: helping me succeed on the pro tour.

And I could've given them much more back.

Old habits die hard, and when I started working with

Andre, I didn't change my ways. I still had plenty of ego from my recent playing career, and now, after all, I was an important part of an important team. And one day, Andre took notice of the way I was acting, and caught me up short.

It happened at a tournament, very early on in our time together. I'd given yet another curt "request" to yet another volunteer worker, and Andre took me aside and told me, in no uncertain terms, that I had to change my ways. "Anything that you do for me is a reflection of me," he said. "When you ask for balls, you say 'please' and 'thank you.' When you ask for a car, be grateful that you got one. Because you're not Brad Gilbert, the tennis player. You're Brad Gilbert coaching Andre Agassi, and you're here with me. And I don't want it coming back to me that you're being rude to people. Get it right. Right now."

My first reaction? Defensive, of course. Thoughts like, *What's he talking about?* And, *Where does he come off?* Well, on count one I immediately saw I didn't have a leg to stand on—the more I thought about it, the more I realized what a jerk I'd been.

As for count two, it now struck me with blunt force that Andre Agassi was the politest guy I had ever met. A lot of people don't buy it: They see him kissing his templed fingers after he wins a match and bowing to the crowd, and think, *Phony.* They see him in a press conference being thoughtful and considerate, and think, *Fake.* It's all too easy, in our cynical time, to believe that this is just another star trying to manipulate his image.

I'm here to tell you, it's no image. A.A.'s dad, Mike, a former Olympic boxer who immigrated here from Iran in 1952, has worked in Las Vegas, for Kirk Kerkorian, since 1959, as a maître d' and casino manager. Mike Agassi's life has been all about service, and he believes in it deeply— for both practical and emotional reasons. Andre told me that when he was a kid, his dad would come home with a whole pocketful of cash from tips, and that money would make the family's life better. So there's one very direct result of superb behavior.

But Andre also observed Mike walking the walk—being genuinely nice to waiters and waitresses, not just to high rollers. Mike truly believed in the Golden Rule. He felt that whatever elevated the people you were dealing with elevated you, too. And that whatever seemed to elevate you while putting down the people you were dealing with really demeaned you. The lesson sank in. Andre's manners are impeccable. And they're not phony; they come from the heart. It drives him crazy, at tennis tournaments, when players throw their old grips and sweaty clothes and dirty towels all over the court, or the locker-room floor. *Somebody is going to have to pick that stuff up*, he thinks. It makes him nuts when people with money boss waiters and waitresses around. And he homed in right away on me, the Poster Child for Behavior Improvement. "I cannot believe you don't pull the chair out for your wife," he told me. "I cannot believe you don't stand up every time she gets up from the table. . . ."

Our work together put Andre into hyperdrive in 1994. He wound up winning five titles, including the U.S. Open, where he was the first unseeded player to win since 1966. He was also the first player, ever, to move from outside the top 30 to number 2 at the end of the year.

I had taught him a few things; he had taught me a few things. But I still had a lot to learn.

> Revise your expectations of who can learn from whom—there's nobody out there who can't teach you an important lesson about something.

All right, I got over myself. Okay, Andre made me get over myself.

Yet day by day, I was also growing a little older and more mature. Chiv had taught me how to be a team player in an individual sport; Andre was teaching me how to be a team *leader* in an individual sport. He had so much wisdom about tennis, and life, that it was tempting, sometimes, to sit back and learn from him.

But he had hired me to be his coach. And I knew from

Chiv that the main purpose of a coach was to see things about his player that the player couldn't see. Or had forgotten to see. Or, in the heat of battle and the day-to-day grind of the tour, had just plain lost sight of.

The more I worked with Andre, the more I realized that even a guy as brilliant as he is—and I mean intellectually as well as in terms of his tennis—could drift off into unproductive territory sometimes. The longer I hung around this strange individual sport of ours, the better I understood that even the greatest need someone to help them hold on to their greatness.

3. You Gotta Love It (Part One)

*How Andre Agassi's insanely positive coach
showed him that a few weeks in the minors wasn't
necessarily a bad thing.*

"You're 141 in the world for no other reason
  than that you've lost your love for tennis.
  It's all about dedicating yourself to training,
  playing, and having a plan."

—*B.G. to Andre Agassi*

Every coach loves to talk about his big successes. I want to tell you what it's like in the trenches.

A player-coach relationship is a little bit like a marriage, and as every husband knows, every marriage has its ups and downs. Andre Agassi and I had an amazing working relationship from 1994 to 2002, and we have a close friendship that continues to this day. And I think we'd both agree that while our friendship has been rock solid the entire way, the greatest tests to our work together came in 1997 and the first half of 1999.

In the spring of 1997 Andre married Brooke Shields. Just as he was trying to get his new marriage on its feet, he found himself in the crosshairs of the world's telephoto lens on a daily basis. Something had to give, and what gave first was his tennis game.

Tennis seemed to be just about the last thing on Andre's mind in 1997. He didn't play the Australian Open in January; he skipped the French Open and Wimbledon. He basically began playing that summer, and he was out of shape physically and mentally—overweight and under-motivated. In the U.S. Open that September, he played Patrick Rafter in the round of 16, and even though Rafter started cramping in the fourth set, Andre wasn't in shape to take advantage of it. He lost the match (and Rafter wound up winning the Open), and we took a month off. Then I thought, *Maybe we should start to build from here.*

His first tourney back was the Eurocard Open in Stuttgart.

Andre's ranking had fallen so low that he had to be wild-carded into Stuttgart that October. His opponent in the first round was Todd Martin. And Andre walked onto that court and proceeded to play one of the most uninspired matches I had ever seen him play. Martin beat him 6–4, 6–4, but it really wasn't even that close. Andre was an absolute shadow of himself out there. After that match was over, Andre Agassi was officially number 141 in the world.

One hundred forty-one! This was a guy who was born to be one of the all-time greats, a guy who had already won Wimbledon and, during our tenure together since 1994, the U.S. Open and the Australian. This was a guy who, at age twenty-seven, I firmly felt, still had greatness in him. And after walking off that court in Stuttgart, Andre looked me in the eye and asked me if I thought he ought to hang it up.

Now, I'd love to be able to give you a Knute Rockne

moment here—but I'm going to have to give you a Brad Gilbert moment instead. Because the truth is that my 1997 with Andre had bummed me out. Had made me feel helpless. What does a coach *do* when his guy is struggling? Some coaches—the kind who say "we won" but "he lost"— split when the chips are down. Some might try to do a little motivational bullying. Neither one is my style. Chiv taught me to be positive in every fiber of my being: If there's anything I want to accomplish in this book, it's to demonstrate that fact to you, to tell you how all-important I feel positiveness is, to show you what it's done for my players and me, and to tell you how I came to be that way.

My job as a coach, my *religion* as a coach, is never, ever, to pass along my bad moods (whatever they happen to be about) to my player. My faith as a coach is to take any situation, no matter how bad it is, and find some positive spin for it. There's no quicker route to crashing and burning than for both player and coach to be down.

And so when Andre looked me in the eye and asked me if I thought it was all over for him, I gave him a little tough love. I said, "You're 141 in the world for no other reason than that you've lost your love for tennis. The game hasn't passed you by. If you put your nose to the grindstone and work your ass off, you can get back to number 1. It's all about dedicating yourself to training, playing, and having a plan. You can't play tennis part time and be great."

And Andre said, "Well, what should we do?"

I told him. Step one, we had to pull him out of the Paris Indoor and all the other tournaments for the rest of the year. He simply wasn't ready to play them, physically or mentally. Step two, he had to go home to Las Vegas and train his ass off—run hills and lift weights under the guidance of his superb trainer Gil Reyes, hit twenty thousand tennis balls with me. Step three, I felt he had to get back into competitive tennis, when he got back in, on a lower level.

It was exactly the same as when a .340 hitter has to go down to Triple-A to regain his stroke a little bit. There are several tiers to the men's pro tennis tour, and somewhere near the bottom are the challenger events—small-money tournaments for wannabes who want to build up enough ATP points to qualify for the main tour. Andre hadn't played a challenger since his first year on the tour, at age sixteen. His first time back was a doozy.

The event was in his hometown, Vegas, in November. Andre won his first four rounds and made it to the final, where he faced one Christian Vinck, a young German who was number 202 in the world. And Vinck, no doubt psyched up for his big chance, played the match of his life. Andre didn't play as well as he could have; Vinck played out of his mind: end of story. Vinck won, 6–4, 7–5.

I have rarely seen Andre so ticked off. "How could I lose

to this guy?" he said—among other things. There's one thing you have to understand about Andre Agassi: Despite his very real manners and humility, he has plenty of ego. You don't have the kind of gifts he has, and do what he's done, without it. If you're engaging in single combat, in very public circumstances, against some of the best athletes in the world, you need to have self-confidence bordering on cockiness to get you through.

At the same time, though, he really is an incredibly intelligent and sensitive man. And so I think his anger after that match had much more to do with disappointment at not living up to his enormous talent than with any kind of contempt for Christian Vinck. After all, Andre was with the program: He never bitched for one second about playing in challengers. When he said, "How can I lose to this guy?" I knew exactly where he was coming from. "Dude, don't worry about it," I told him. "We got five matches in this week—let's go to Burbank next week and get after it." Burbank, of course, being the site of the next challenger tournament.

Andre couldn't believe that I could spin his loss in Vegas into a positive. (Sometimes I even surprise myself.) But what did he do next? He went to Burbank and won—counting the loss to Vinck, he wound up winning nine out of ten matches in two weeks. The minor leagues were working for him. At the end of 1997, he had raised his ranking to number 105 in the world—not spectacular, but a start. "Let's hit the ground running in 1998," I told him, "and get things going."

Now, the Knute Rockne version of the story would be if Andre started knocking off tournament after tournament in 1998—can't you just see the movie montage of him raising the champion's cups at the French, Wimbledon, and the U.S. Open?

Life isn't a movie. Andre played very well in 1998—by the end of the year, his ranking had gone up 99 places to number 6—but for whatever reason, he didn't play well in the major tournaments. At the Australian Open, he lost a tough five-setter to Alberto Berasategui of Spain—the first time Andre had ever lost a match after being up two sets to none. At the French, he lost another five-setter to an up-and-coming Russian genius named Marat Safin—just a bad first-round draw. At Wimbledon, he was tinkering with a different racquet. Tommy Haas sent him out in the second round. So A.A. went back to his old stick, and raised his game all summer: won in Washington and L.A.; got to the semis in Montreal.

Then he lost still another five-setter to Karol Kucera at the U.S. Open.

So much for Knute Rockne.

Well, you know what? I thought that in every one of those majors he lost, he was better than the guy he lost to—but I also didn't think it was the end of the world. When Andre and I talked about his 1998, we decided that he had to get back to doing well in the majors again. He had to do things differently.

But what?

> Personal ambition is the cart, enthusiasm is the horse. Put the horse in front, and everyone will want to jump onto your cart.

All athletes play with pain. Most of the time you work through it—I spent most of my playing career working through it—but sometimes it stops you cold. And once you're sidelined, it's rough. Not too many people care about you but yourself. I've always said the pro tennis tour is like a treadmill: If you fall off, it just keeps on going. And it's hard as hell to climb back on.

Andre's always been a guy who's in tune with his whole life, not just the tennis part—and when the nontennis part got out of whack, his body did, too. Then he put his pride aside, went down to the minors, and made regaining his love for the game a priority. Admirable. He worked his ass off, and he got results.

But his body still kept giving him trouble.

A huge part of my job is trying to see through my guy's eyes. A less-known part of the gig is being able to step back and see the guy in a way he can't see himself. When

Andre's body and spirit were both so banged up that he felt he just had to stop playing for a while, I found myself (to my surprise) disagreeing with him. This had nothing to do with my pride, or his. It was all about reaching the goal we'd set out to attain together.

4. You Gotta Love It (Part Two)

How the impossible can turn possible, in four or five not-so-easy steps.

"I can't believe you got me to do this."
   —*Andre Agassi to B.G., about the 1999 French Open*

E ven though Andre came out of the gate swinging in 1999, hitting the ball better than he had for a long time, his mind was divided. He was going through a difficult time off the court, even as he was trying to climb back up the mountain to number 1.

At the same time, his body was beginning to talk back to him a little bit. On the men's tour, after a certain point, it doesn't matter how hard you train and what kind of shape you're in—the relentless grind of banging around on those courts week after week starts to get into your muscles and joints. And when you're in a certain amount of emotional turmoil, your body is vulnerable.

In March, in Scottsdale, Arizona, Andre had to default against Jan-Michael Gambill in the semis when he hurt his hip. He took three weeks off, and when he came back, he was hitting the ball better than I'd ever seen him hit it. *He's back,* I thought.

Then we went to the Far East.

In the final at Hong Kong, in April, Andre played Boris

Becker, and there were about five rain delays over a two-day period. Starting and stopping is always tough on the body, and when they finally finished the match—which Andre won—his shoulder was killing him.

We were supposed to go on to Tokyo, and then kick off the clay-court season in Monte Carlo, as part of the run up to the French Open at the end of May. Instead we had to pull out of both Tokyo and Monte Carlo and take a month off. We came back for Rome at the beginning of May, but Andre's shoulder was still giving him trouble. It was the first time I'd seen him struggle because of problems with the arm, and I could tell it was kind of playing with his head—along with the other things that were playing in there. He lost, third round, to Patrick Rafter.

We were at an impasse. The shoulder really was bothering him. Should he go home and rest it? Should he stay in Europe and try to play it out? There were two weeks before the French. In the back of both our minds, I'm sure, were those two lost French finals, in 1990 and 1991. Even though I'm a firm believer in never dwelling on the past—it ain't coming back!—there was no getting around the fact that Andre was twenty-nine now, and he only had so many French Opens left. You don't just blow one off lightly. And if he returned home to Vegas now, he wouldn't come back to Europe that season—not for the French, not for Wimbledon.

There was a team championship in Dusseldorf five days

later, on clay, the week before Roland Garros. I thought the shoulder might calm down in five days. I said, "Let's go to Dusseldorf; they need an extra guy." Andre didn't look very certain when he said okay.

His shoulder started hurting so badly in the middle of the first set of his first match that he walked off the court, a default. He couldn't serve.

He was in a black mood—the worst mood I've ever seen him in. "That's it," Andre said. "We're leaving, and we're not coming back. I'm not playing the French—pull me out."

But something was nagging at me: My gut was telling me not to throw in the towel. "I'm not going to do that, dude," I told him. "We're going to be able to play the French."

Andre looked me square in the eye and shook his head. "No, we're not," he said.

To get back to the States from Dusseldorf you have to take Lufthansa Flight 454 via Frankfurt. Andre and I have taken that flight so many times, but this time was a little worse than all the others. We'd gone out and had a few drinks the night before, I guess to try and get our minds off the fact that our 1999 season seemed to be going off the rails. (If not down the tubes.)

It was early on a Monday morning, and we were both a little ornery. Andre kept saying, "I'll be right for the summer hard courts." But I had this weird bug in my brain that wouldn't stop buzzing. Maybe it was inspiration; maybe it was the hangover. I said, "No, we'll be back in Paris in six days. You're going to go see Lenny—Lenny's going to take care of you."

We were flying to San Francisco. I live in Marin County, about a half hour north of the city; Andre was going to catch a connecting flight home to Vegas. But I really didn't want him to go to Vegas; I wanted him to see Lenny Stein. Lenny is a friend of mine in San Francisco, a chiropractor—at least, that's what it says on his shingle. I think of him as a magician.

So we're staggering onto the plane in Frankfurt, red-eyed, whiskery, grousing at each other like an old married couple. "Ah, no one guy is going to make me feel better," Andre kept saying.

"I'm telling you, stay at my place for the week," I kept saying. "Lenny'll work on the shoulder four days, twice a day. It's going to be fine." But he didn't want to hear it.

Andre's bad mood about his shoulder kept getting worse. He had a ten-hour flight ahead of him, and he couldn't get to sleep. He just wanted to shut out the world for a little while—not to mention me, bugging him.

He had a vodka and orange juice. Then he had another.

Meanwhile, I was still trying to talk up Lenny and the French Open. (As you may have noticed, once I get started on a subject, there's no letup.)

"Ah, I don't want to listen to you," Andre said. And finally fell asleep.

He slept for nine hours. I stayed awake the whole flight, thinking. And when Andre woke up, I picked up my rap right where I had left off. "You're not going to Vegas," I told him.

He was groggy. "You're not still on that, are you?" he said.

"Yup," I said.

When we got off the plane, I said, "We're going to my place."

Andre said, "But you pulled me out of the French already, right?" As soon as he walked off the court in Dusseldorf, he had told me to pull him out of everything for the next three months. Of course, I didn't do it—for one thing, the deadline for withdrawing from the French, which started the following Monday, wasn't until the Tuesday before.

"No," I said. "I didn't pull you out of the French."

Big sigh from Andre. "All right, listen," he said. "I'm tired of you being on me—I'll come over to your place and see Kimmie and the kids and stay in the guest cottage for a day."

I hadn't just been thinking while Andre slept on the

plane. I'd also been doing a little off-court strategizing. I phoned Kim mid-flight and told her I was bringing Andre home. "Go grocery shopping, get something good," I told her. "I want to keep him around for a few days."

We got to my place that afternoon, and Lenny did a treatment on him that night. Then two more treatments on Tuesday, Wednesday, and Thursday, and one on Friday morning. On Tuesday, Lenny said, "I'm telling you, the shoulder's getting a little better." On Wednesday he said, "Some of the tightness is still there, but it's better."

But that same day, Andre was still telling me he wouldn't be able to play. And I told him, "Listen, let's just do what we can. Because if we don't go to the 1999 French, you can't win it. You can never get it back. But if we go there, you just never know. Something good could happen. Lightning could strike. You just never know."

On Thursday we hit on my hard court for ten minutes— no serving, just ground strokes—and Andre looked surprised. "Huh," he said. "It's feeling better." And after the treatment on Friday morning, Lenny said, "I wouldn't be surprised if he's 95 percent in two days."

We hit for another thirty minutes after that Friday treatment, and Andre smiled. "I'm going to be okay," he said. "It feels okay."

On Friday night, as we boarded the plane for Paris, Andre turned and gave me a look. "I can't believe you got me to do this," he told me.

On Saturday we did a full practice at Roland Garros. Andre looked good; he was almost totally back to normal. He could serve with no pain. But I was still worried: He hadn't played a match since losing to Rafter in Rome.

And his first-round opponent was an Argentinean named Franco Squillari. "Oh my God," I said. "The dirt rat of dirt rats."

The French Open is played on slow red clay, a surface that Spaniards and South Americans have a particular love for. I knew a little bit about Squillari and his record on clay. He was ranked around 25 in the world, a dangerous floater in the draw. I had a hunch Andre was in for a brutal first-round match.

When I watched Squillari practice on Sunday, my fears were confirmed. This guy had a *huge* forehand, and he ran around every backhand to hit a putaway with his money shot. He ran down everything—and on the slow clay, a lot more balls can be run down. He was the dirt-baller supreme. A very rough first round when your confidence is down.

The match started late Monday afternoon, on the stadium court, with a full crowd: Andre's hugely popular in France. And right out of the gate, Squillari was playing unbelievably well. I thought Andre played damn well in the first set, given the fact that the stadium was full and he wasn't exactly match tough—and Squillari won the set, 6–3. I'm sitting in the stands, trying to keep a calm face for Andre, but I'm thinking, "God, if this guy keeps it up, Andre's going to get hammered, and he's going to give me that look—*I can't believe we came back for this.*"

In the second set he got in trouble at 4–all, and then again at 5–all, then he somehow managed to win the set 7–5. The level of tennis was unbelievable. It shocked me that Andre could play this well without having competed for weeks, without having trained at all for the past week. And then there was the fact that he was coming off this injury, and playing a guy that was playing tremendous tennis.

And the third set was even rougher. Squillari broke Andre's serve, and Andre fell behind—and then, somehow, he was able to break back, hold serve, and break again. When he won the third, 7–5, the crowd gave Andre a standing ovation. But as I stared down at him—the sun was setting and the air was getting cold—I was wondering how he was going to physically get through one, and maybe two, more sets.

Then, at the beginning of the next set, Squillari cramped. I blinked in amazement. Andre won the set 6–3, and with it, his first-round match.

Andre was as excited as if he'd won the tournament. "I can't believe *I* made that dude quit," he said. I almost gave him my Chiv speech—"Let's not get too worked up; one round at a time." But what I was beginning to learn was that one size does not fit all: A similar situation is not the same situation. The other lesson I was taking in was to watch my man very carefully, to read his cues and think before I opened my mouth. And right now, I could see that Andre truly needed to be pumped up. In his mind, he had come from off the radar screen to being in this tournament. He'd just played for three hours and twenty minutes. His shoulder had held, his body and mind had held. That was everything we could ask for. I remember I'd had a little speech all ready if Andre had lost that epic battle. "You know what?" I would've said. "You gave yourself a shot. You did everything you could. You fought through it."

I didn't have to make the speech. Yet.

Andre has always been a great front-runner, a less-than-great come-from-behind player. That's been true of several of the tennis giants, and the main reason they get away with it is that they just don't have to come from behind very often.

In the 1999 French Open, Andre had to dig himself out of serious holes four times.

In the second round, he played a Frenchman named Arnaud Clément. The weather was hot, the clay was dry, the balls were (comparatively) light. Perfect conditions for Andre. So he wins the first set easily, 6–2, and he's absolutely rolling, playing like a genius. Now he's up a ser-

vice break in the second, and he's making it look so ef-
fortless, moving Clément left, right, left, right, that the
crowd is almost laughing. Then Andre jokes with the
crowd, and actually *gets* them laughing.

And then, somehow, it was as if somebody had thrown a
light switch. The next thing you know, Andre's game started
going down, down, down, and Clément's game started going up, up, up. Andre was up 4–2 in the second set, and
wound up losing four games in a row. The match is all even,
and I'm sitting there thinking, "What the hell happened?"

Then Andre lost the third set, 6–2. Several times, I could
tell he was a little fatigued and struggling with his game.
And now he was down two sets to one. The whole time,
he was looking over at me, and I was just trying to be
positive—to give him a sense of, *Come on, hang in there.* But
meanwhile the crowd was in a frenzy, because while they
may love Andre, this was a French guy he was playing, and
the French guy was putting up a real fight!

The fourth set went to 5–5, then Clément held serve to
go ahead 6–5. Andre was about to serve to stay in the
match. But as they changed ends, as Clément walked to
his chair, I turned to Gil, Andre's trainer, and said, "I
think the guy is cramping." Gil said, "You think?" I nodded. And Gil looked hard at Clément and said, "You're
right." Clément was clutching his leg and calling for the
trainer. Here he is, one game from the finish line, and
he's getting worked on by the trainer. Three-minute delay.

I always look calm out there. First of all, it's my *job* to look calm; my players depend on me for it. And I'm fortunate enough to have a face with a steady look about it.

But the truth is (don't tell Andy, okay?) that often as not, I'm dying a thousand deaths out there. I understand the heat of battle all too well. I know how flukey a tennis match can get, how a fickle crowd that wants to see more tennis can turn a sure win into an epic struggle. When you're the player on the court, you have some power to control all this. When you're the coach in the stands, and all you have is the strength of your face and the hope that your guy remembers all the prematch strategizing, well . . . that's when you really earn your dough.

Clément was limping when he came back out to receive Andre's serve, and I was dying. Andre is one game from losing, yet he has this guy in a sleeper hold. The guy is all but paralyzed. But on Clément's first two service returns, Andre nets a backhand, then sails a forehand. In two points, the French is going to be all over for him.

Then Andre plays four solid points on his serve and wins the game to force a tiebreaker. I'm sitting there thinking, *Just tough this out; tough this out, and everything is going to be fine.* And sure enough, Andre toughs the tiebreaker out, and the fourth set is his. Clément was officially out of gas: Andre won the final set 6–0.

In another situation, Andre might've been pretty peeved after that match. He might've walked into the locker room scowling after having held on by his fingernails against yet another guy he should have beaten a lot more easily that day.

Instead, he was even more excited than he was after the Squillari match. Here he was, supposedly out of shape, having just made two very fit guys cramp. Having made a guy two points from winning say "uncle."

At this point I really did have to put on my Chiv cap and calm Andre down. "Let's just think about the next match, okay?" I said.

Fortunately we didn't have to think too much. Every once in a while, even in the third round of a Grand Slam, you get a nice draw. Chris Woodruff had beaten Andre the one previous time they'd played, but he wasn't truly a clay courter, and he was a little sore from his previous match. Andre hammered him in straight sets, and we were into the second week. In the thick of things. And Andre hadn't been in the thick of things in the French since 1995. A long dry spell.

And his next opponent, in the round of 16, was the defending champion, Carlos Moya.

After three rounds, Andre finally felt he really had his game on again. Unfortunately, Andre has had a little trouble playing Spanish guys on the clay courts: The heavy spin and the slowness of the ball work against him. Fortunately, after three rounds of Agassi-friendly conditions, the hot and dry weather continued keeping the court quicker. But from the moment Moya stepped on the court, the Spaniard was on fire. Serving big, cracking his forehand, he won the first set easily, 6–4. Andre looked up at me a couple of times, and I could read his eyes: *I don't know if I'm going to get this guy today.*

I had to disagree with him: It's my job. "Keep fighting!" I yelled. "Just keep working!" But his shoulders were a little slumped, and I was worried. It was the second set, Andre was on my side of the court, and he lost his serve for the second time to go down 1–4. Bad news. Down 6–4, 4–1, double break to the defending champ. Very bad news.

Moya was still playing unbelievable tennis, and Andre still had that look. He was rushing—like he was in a hurry to get it all over with. I always keep it deep down inside, but sometimes I just think, *You know what? He's not going to get through this guy today. I don't know, somehow he didn't peak for it.* This was one of those times.

And just then, as if somebody had thrown that same light switch from the Clément match, only in reverse, things turned around. Suddenly—I guess because he was nearly out of it, with nothing to lose—Andre just started hitting out, loosening up, playing much more aggressively. And just as suddenly, out of nowhere, Moya double-faulted a couple of times in that 4–1 game. He hadn't double-faulted at all up till then. Now he played a couple of loose points, and between his looseness and Andre tightening the reins, the next thing you know, this match had turned around.

Andre won four straight games, Moya won one, then Andre closed out the set, 7–5. He gave a little fist pump then, not a big one: What it said to me was, *I'm in it. I can't believe this. Ten minutes ago I was down 6–4, 4–1, double break; I was out of it, done.*

He went down an early break, but wound up winning an unbelievably tense third set. The crowd was like a sleeping giant in that set—they woke up and made Andre their honorary Frenchman for the afternoon, rallying him back to life. Then somehow, Moya just snapped. His spirit was crushed, and Andre ran through him in the fourth set, 6–1. When we got into the locker room afterwards, Andre grinned at me. "Man, we've been through this three times already, from the brink," he said, shaking his head.

"It's fate," I told him.

"Or something," he said.

What it really was was guts. He dug his way out of jail three out of four times against guys who were playing well, and all of a sudden, found something in himself that made him a better player than he'd ever been before. Part of my philosophy about being great is this: When you do get out of jail, you have to have the genius quality to take advantage of the opportunity. Sometimes, when you gut out that ugly match, fate sends you a little bonus the next day—a bonus you wouldn't have been around for if you hadn't been able to capitalize.

That was exactly what happened in the quarterfinals. This time, what fate sent us was Marcelo Filippini, a Uruguayan qualifier who was coming off a gruesome battle against Greg Rusedski. Filippini was so out of gas that Andre beat him in an hour and ten minutes, 6–2, 6–2, 6–0.

It felt as though we'd stepped out of the clouds and into the clear sunlight, just below the summit of the mountain. Andre had lost the 1990 and 1991 finals here, which had been his to win. Maybe he thought he was never going to win the French. But all at once he was in the semis, and all three of the other guys—his opponent, Dominik Hrbaty of Slovakia; and on the other side, Fernando Meligeni of Brazil and Andrei Medvedev of the Ukraine—were unseeded, and Andre, at number 13, the only one who'd won a major before, was the clear-cut favorite.

It had been raining on and off for a couple of days, the tournament was behind schedule (remember the 2003 U.S. Open?), and Andre was worried he'd have to play too many matches in too few days.

He won the first set against Hrbaty, then it started to rain. Andre won the second set in the rain, then lost the third in the mud. Then they stopped the match. In the locker room he told me, "It was so heavy out there, my arm was getting tired. I felt lucky they stopped it." The court had been playing slow as molasses.

I was beginning to discover that I did my best coaching when we were both relaxed, and that the best time of all was dinner. The name I came up with for it was Vittles the Night Before. Intensity is fine in its place. But when you're sitting in a fine restaurant (and finding some of the best restaurants in the world is one of my favorite parts about my job), with a beer in your hand, it's a great time to bring up a little bit about tomorrow. I was realizing that that was when I did some of my best work.

That night we were in my favorite Paris restaurant, Le Stresa, which made my usual tendency to put a positive spin on everything even easier. I said, "I'm telling you, we're going to have good weather tomorrow. You're going to run through this guy in twenty minutes."

Andre gave me that look he'd sometimes give me, like, *Easy for you to say.* But once I get positive, I won't let anything stop me. "I'm telling you," I said. "It's going to be perfect—we're going to get through this guy in twenty minutes tomorrow."

Sure enough, the sun came out the next day, Andre broke Hrbaty's serve once, and won in twenty-four minutes. Talk about the power of positive thinking!

We were in the finals, and Gil and I were excited, to say the least. After all Andre had gone through, from 1997 to this moment! But I couldn't think about any of that. The moment the match was over, I was consumed with strategizing against Meligeni and Medvedev's games. Which one would it be? Then Medvedev won. I barely slept that night—I was counting X's and O's instead of sheep.

Andrei Medvedev was number 4 in the world, the hot young guy on the tour—and he was having an absolutely terrible year. He had lost something like seven first rounders in a row; before the French, he hadn't won a match since Key Biscayne. His confidence had been shot.

But here he was picking it up. He beat Sampras in the second round, and carried it through to the final. He was a good clay courter. Still, none of this mattered to me. I thought Andre was going to roll over the guy. I told him, "If you just go out there and take care of business, execute what you've been doing, play aggressive and work him, and watch his backhand down the line, you'll win this."

But there's a kind of rule in tennis: You never know what's going to happen until you walk onto the court. I like to say, *Two men enter, one man leaves.* And Andre went out to play that final, and—I had never seen this before from him, ever—it was as if the body, the mind—everything—froze up. Nobody was home. He lost the first two sets, 6–1, 6–2, in forty minutes. And in the first game of the third set, he was lucky as hell to hold serve.

Gil kept asking me, "What's going on? What's happening?" I shrugged helplessly. I had no idea. I kept thinking, *He's not playing*, but I couldn't figure out why. Was it nerves? Andre just wasn't there. And then came another act of God: It started to rain.

It was one game all in the third set. I thought, *Come on, just rain a little harder; we just need to stop play; we've* got *to stop play.* Andre was looking up at me, and I kept motioning: *Tell the umpire to stop.*

Then Andre went up to the umpire and asked him to stop, and the umpire called the tournament director on his walkie-talkie, and they did stop play. Medvedev was upset: Momentum was on his side.

Andre went into the locker room. I let him have a minute in there by himself. Then I went in.

A million thoughts were going through my head. Part of me was thrilled that we'd gotten the break—*something* had to change. And another part of me was relieved at having the chance to talk to Andre and find out what the hell was going on.

The first thing he said to me was, "The guy is too good—I just can't beat him today. He's just playing too well."

That stopped me in my tracks for a second. I looked at him and said, "Andre, what are you doing? You've worked so hard to get here. If you're going to lose, lose with your guns blazing. Go back on that frickin' court and start playing. Start hitting the ball and start dictating play. And if you lose, make him hit the shots. Make him earn it. Make him win it. Go out there and beat this guy. This guy is not better than you. If this guy is better than you, I'll die right here. He's *not* better than you. You're just not playing. Go play your game." And I turned and walked out.

It might've been the shortest rain delay ever. Four, five minutes, tops. Amazing luck—in effect, I'd been given the chance to call my own time-out. Andre and Medvedev battled to 4–all. But now, even though Andre still hadn't broken Medvedev's serve, he was at least dictating play. He was making errors, but going for his shots, and the match was starting to be more at his pace.

And Andre was starting to find his game—just. Serving at 4–all, he saved a break point with a miraculous scoop volley that literally rolled over the net tape, and Medvedev could barely get his racquet on it. If Andre hadn't hit that volley, Medvedev would've been serving for the match.

Andre hadn't come close to breaking Medvedev's serve the entire match. But after that volley, Andre held serve, and for the first time, I noticed that Medvedev was shrugging his shoulders a little bit. And when Andre changed ends, he did a little skip step over to his chair. Have you ever noticed that little chatter step he does while he's sitting on the changeover? I smiled. I know my guy, and I know that when the skip step is back, so is his confidence.

Andre broke Medvedev's serve to take the third set, 6–4. Now he had a little fire in his belly, and all at once, so did the crowd. The stands woke up and got on Andre's side. And between that fire in his belly and the reenergized crowd, he started hitting the ball the way he had the whole tourney—ripping everything, taking every shot early, completely dominating play.

Fourth set, Agassi, six games to three.

Andre broke Medvedev's serve early in the fifth and deciding set, but Medvedev didn't fold. When he served at 3–5, he had to fight off four match points, and he saved all four with great first serves. Five games to four, Agassi. When they switched sides, Andre passed my seat, and I yelled, "You just got to believe! Four points!"

Which is exactly what Andre did. He closed out the match with a serve and a winner and then three service winners. When he held up that cup, with tears in his eyes, it was like he'd been reborn.

Good thing we went.

> Certain defeat is only certain to stagnant minds.

We all have our limits, but no matter how smart we are (and almost no matter how optimistic we are), we don't really have any idea exactly where those limits lie. As smart and as tough as Andre is—and he's very smart, and very tough—he firmly believed that there was no way he could even go to the 1999 French Open, let alone win it.

He needed my belief in him and my goading to get there, and to get through.

Stay with me on this one: I believe it took a certain arrogance on Andre's part to feel he knew where his limits lay before that tournament. And it took a certain humility on his part to yield to my persuasion, to come to my place instead of going home, to accept help from me and Dr. Lenny Stein. That humility put Andre in a position to exceed what he had thought were his limits, and to be his very best.

A player and his or her coach have a common goal: for the player to win. Both player and coach have to invest a certain amount of humility into that quest. If one or the other is arrogant, if there's any kind of power struggle between them, their relationship will very quickly be history.

It's a complicated relationship. In a team sport, players and coach get paid by the same person. In tennis, one person signs the other's checks, one gives the other instructions—if there's any resentment about roles, it festers fast. The only way through all of it (in my opinion, anyway) is for the player and coach to relax together, to share off-court time, to have fun. The ability to laugh at the same things is essential.

Early on with Andre, I came up with the idea of making no-lose bets on his results in big tournaments. If he didn't win the title, nothing happened. But if he did, I had to do something I didn't especially want to do—get an earring, for example.

It was a way of being in it with him. It was a lot more fun and interesting than betting money. It gave me my own chance to be humble in pursuit of our goal. It cemented us as a team. And it pushed my own limits, helped me avoid getting stagnant or complacent.

As I would learn, though, there are limits and there are limits.

5. Why You, Too, Should Try Skydiving

Belief is a huge thing. If you don't believe it, you're not going to do it. If you believe it, you've got a great shot.

"Brad—I don't win matches on grass."

> —*Andy Roddick to B.G., just before winning ten matches in a row, on grass, at Queen's and Wimbledon in 2003*

L ife is full of surprises: Some are bad, a few are good. And with some, it takes a while to figure out just what the hell they are.

In January of 2002, Andre reinjured his wrist and dropped out of the Australian Open. We both went home. Andre took a couple of weeks off with Steffi and their new baby son, and when he got back I called and invited him out to breakfast. I didn't have anything special to discuss; I just wanted to see my friend.

We talked about a lot of things that morning, personal and business, and as we sat in my living room, we got to discussing our work together. It's the kind of chat that's good to have once in a while, on an informal basis, just so nobody's taking anything for granted. Andre was in a philosophical mood that day: He'd been spooked at first about hurting his wrist and not being able to defend his 2001 Aussie title, but now he was looking to the year ahead. Suddenly it occurred to him that maybe he needed a new voice.

Before I knew it, we were contemplating a change in Andre's coaching situation.

I don't remember who brought it up first, but it came out of a positive rather than a negative place. We had had an amazing eight-year run together, in the course of which Andre had gone from as low as number 141 in the world to his rightful place at and near the top of the rankings. We were close friends, our affection and respect for each other intact after many tests. We had disagreed many times, but we had never spoken an angry word to each other. Change makes people grow: Maybe it was time to shake things up a bit.

Just as you don't want to let a marriage get stale, you don't want a coaching situation to drift along on auto-pilot. And right now, it looked as if Andre and I had the opportunity to keep on being friends, and avoid our business relationship's getting stale.

Andre knew how much I loved Kim and our three kids, and the truth is that after eight years of traveling over thirty weeks a year, I was beginning to feel a little selfish. With my financial success tied to Andre's, I had done very well. I was providing nicely for my family. But my family needed *me.*

By the time Andre and I stood up from that breakfast table, we were smiling and giving each other a manly hug. Now we could concentrate totally on our friendship.

· · ·

There's no balance in a career like mine—not that there are many careers like mine! I may have a tennis court a stone's throw from my kitchen window, but I can't coach a great player in my backyard. The professional tennis tour is a movable feast. Either you move with it, or you're off the job.

After twenty years of travel as a player and then a coach, twenty years of living out of suitcases and equipment bags, I went home. I would wind up staying there for fifteen months, and loving every minute. I had just turned forty, and I was finally getting a chance to smell the roses. (Kim, who has a major green thumb, planted those roses.) I got to drive my kids to school; I got to greet them when they came home. I got to go out for romantic dinners with Kim. We all went on family vacations.

Now, this is not to say that this neurotic Jewish guy went all mellow overnight. I've never been the world's finest sleeper, and even off the tour, I'd find myself waking up at three A.M., my brain revving into the red zone—only now, instead of obsessing about Andre's next opponent's cross-court backhand, I kept thinking about my life.

Forty, after all, is the gateway to middle age, and I was having those kind of gateway thoughts. Would I go back to coaching? After all my success with Andre, there were certainly feelers, from some very talented tennis players, but somehow the fit never felt exactly right. As you may have begun to realize, I'm pretty fussy about who I work with. (It's nice to have that luxury!) Yes, I'm looking for players with the potential to be great. But first and foremost for me—always—is the personal fit. Whoever I coach has to be somebody I like a lot, someone I feel pretty happy about spending most of my waking hours with. Since I give my heart and soul to my work, I don't want to feel like I'm punching a time clock when the day's work is done.

I've always been a guy who follows all sports avidly, but naturally I pay especially close attention to the men's tennis tour. And one guy I couldn't help being very aware of over the last couple of years was Andy Roddick. I thought all the talk about Andy's being the future of American tennis wasn't just hype: I'd seen the guy play, and as with Andre, I felt his potential was infinite. Sure, there were parts of his game he needed to work on, but that only made him more interesting.

I'd also met Andy, and I'd liked him a lot. He was a big, strong kid with a good head on his shoulders and a wicked sense of humor—about himself as well as everyone else. He was an amazing mimic—his Ozzy Osbourne was dead on—and he also had an incredible gift for imitating other tennis players. He could do Sampras's serve, Andre's forehand, and the Frenchman Fabrice Santoro's drop shot. As I would soon learn, you had to be careful around him: If he saw you just walk across the room, a moment later he could imitate that walk well enough to make your friends howl with laughter.

A coach never stops coaching, even when he's not coaching, and as a sharp-eyed watcher of tennis (an *attention payer*) I thought all the time about what I could do for various players on the tour. Call it a hobby; call it an obsession. Andy was one guy I thought about a lot. At the beginning of 2003, he was number 10 in the world, and he was losing some key matches to guys I thought he shouldn't be losing to. *I could do something for him*, I thought.

But the thing is, Andy already had a coach. Since the beginning of his pro career he'd been working with a former pro named Tarik Benhabiles. Tarik's French/Algerian, a small, very intense guy—a totally different cat from me, Mr. Positive here. (Although I would say that what we have in common is being intensely competitive. We just go at it in different ways.)

Anyway, even though I felt Andy wasn't playing up to his potential, I gave Tarik the benefit of the doubt. Maybe, I thought, things would fall into place for Andy and him. I knew I'd love to work with Andy, but early in 2003, I felt it just wasn't in the cards. Maybe somewhere down the line, I thought, as I drove my little truck out to the dump to get yet another load of dirt for Kim's garden. Or maybe not.

When the French Open began that May, I followed it with particular interest. For one thing, I wondered how

Andre (who'd hired Darren Cahill as his new coach, and started the year by winning the Australian Open for the fourth time) would do. But I also had one eye on Andy Roddick, who was seeded 6th.

And who proceeded to lose in the first round to the un-seeded Sargis Sargsian, of Armenia.

Now, this is nothing against Sargis, who's a solid top-40 player. But I knew Andy had greatness in him. I couldn't help thinking, "God, that was a surprising loss." Andy was in fine physical shape, as far as I knew. I had to wonder what was going on in his head.

That was on the first Tuesday of the French. On Saturday morning, about seven-thirty, I took my truck to the dump to pick up another load of planting dirt for Kim. When I got home, at around nine, my beautiful wife had a funny look on her face.

"Andy Roddick called," she told me.

"Really?" I said. "That's pretty interesting."

Actually, as I later reconstructed it, he had called twice. The first time he phoned, my six-year-old, Zoe answered. "Dad's not home," she told Andy Roddick, and hung up.

Then Andy was patient enough to call back twenty minutes later. Fortunately, this time he got Kim. He called her Mrs. Gilbert.

"Sounds like he wants to talk," she said. "He sounded really excited."

So I phoned Andy back.

"How are you doing?" I asked him.

"Not so great," he said.

I said a few words about my playing days, talked about losing to players I should have beaten. "It's always tough," I told Andy. "But the year isn't even halfway over—plenty of events left to go."

"Listen," Andy said. "I'm thinking about making a move. It's time. Would you be interested?"

And literally, without thinking about it, I said, "I'll be there tomorrow."

I knew I could take him to another level.

I met Andy in London, where he was about to prepare for Queen's—the grass-court tournament at Queen's Club that's a tune-up for Wimbledon, eight days later. He couldn't have been in a more negative frame of mind. For one thing, he was coming off that confidence-killing first-rounder in the French. For another, he had just fired his old coach. Andy doesn't get enough credit for the fact that he got on a train, went to Paris, and told Tarik the news in person; 99.9 percent of touring pros would've done it over the phone. Or by e-mail. Or had someone else do it. Not Andy—he's what we Jews call a mensch. A grown-up in a 20-year-old body. But his first coach had taken him a long way, and it still hurt Andy to do it.

And for another thing, Andy Roddick was convinced—

and I mean completely convinced—that he couldn't win sets, let alone matches, on grass. He had a terrible record on the surface, and a terrible attitude about playing on it.

My question was, *Which came first?*

And so the very first thing I said to him was, "You're going to go 12–0 here on the grass." Meaning, he would win all five matches at Queen's, then all seven at Wimbledon. Meaning he would win both tournaments.

He gave me a funny look—part disbelieving, part wanting to believe. "Brad—I don't win many matches on the grass," he said.

"Dude," I answered, "read my lips. You're going to go 12–0."

The first thing I needed to make Andy understand—really understand—was that it was now Day One. His lousy record on grass didn't matter. The first-round loss at the French didn't matter. His tendency to lose his temper at critical moments and blow matches didn't matter. That was all in the past, and the past was never coming back. All that was about to change. Right now.

I looked at Andy and smiled. "Let's go to work," I told him. "Good things will happen."

Now he was smiling a little bit. I could see the wanting-to-believe part of him was getting the edge.

I said, "Listen, you're going to love grass. You serve huge, you have a great forehand. This surface is *designed* for you to play well."

He was thinking about it.

"You can put a negative spin on anything if you work on it hard enough," I said. "You can talk yourself out of anything. But I'd like to think that you can talk yourself into anything. Belief is a huge thing. If you don't believe it, you're not going to do it. If you believe it, you've got a great shot."

His smile had gotten a lot wider.

Before I tell you what happened at Queen's and Wimbledon, I want to relate a small detail about my first practice with Andy. He walked out onto the court carrying his big equipment bag and wearing an orange visor, backward, with the bill flipped up. He'd spiked his hair with gel. All very hip-hop.

I'd seen that orange visor before, and I didn't like it. Except that now I was his coach.

Why didn't I like the visor? Maybe it was partly a generational thing, but mostly it wasn't. Mostly it was that I found the visor unintimidating. No, not just unintimidating—the opposite of intimidating.

Andre once did a camera commercial where he said, "Image is everything." I don't know if I'd quite go that far, but image is a lot more important in professional sports than you might imagine. I grew up in the Bay Area, and I've been a huge Oakland Raiders fan from a very young age. And one thing that always impressed me about the Raiders, from their tough-guy owner Al Davis on down, was the menacing image they conveyed. I loved the black jerseys (black became my favorite color when I played and coached); I loved the team logo, that eyepatch-wearing football player on a background of crossed swords. There was a little bit of humor to it, but mostly what it said was, "We are going to fight, and we are going to win, because we are the toughest SOBs out there."

Now, tennis isn't pro football—in our sport you get fined, rather than rewarded, for physical contact. But men's professional tennis, while it is entertainment, is also a form of single combat, a kind of gladiatorial contest. You're out there fighting the other guy for a paycheck, for a chance to live a better life and maybe send some kids through college. He's out there to take the money out of your hands. You don't see tennis pros making chitchat when they change sides during a match. Sometimes, I can tell you from personal experience, there's even a little trash-talking out there. ("You don't deserve to be on the same court with me," John McEnroe told me during our match at the 1986 Masters. That day anyway, since I beat him pretty soundly, I guess I did deserve it.)

Tennis pros might laugh and have a couple of beers after a match. But it's war out on the court, and my feeling has always been, *You'd better look like you're ready to do battle.*

An orange visor, backward, with a flipped-up bill, didn't

look very warlike to me. Andy's a big guy, with a big game. You want to build on your strengths, not take away from them. I told him, "This thing does not look physical, dude. You're just not going to beat somebody in a big match wearing an orange visor. Just do me a favor and get rid of that thing."

He got rid of it.

Oh, and as for Queen's and Wimbledon: Andy only went 10–1. The eventual Wimbledon champion, Roger Federer, stopped him in the semis there. But at Queen's, Andy won the tournament (and beat Andre in the semis).

Not too shabby for a guy who can't play on grass.

This is reminding me of something. Back when I spent that one semester at Pepperdine, preparing for the NCAA Championships, my great and nutty coach Allen Fox took it into his head that he wanted me to become more of a net player. Great—except for one thing. I was a rallyer, a baseline player. And I was pretty good at it: Nobody was beating me much in collegiate competition. But Allen was looking into my future. I couldn't see that far yet. "Foxy, I can't volley," I told him.

Foxy, I can't volley. Talk about waving a red flag in front of a bull!

Allen laughed at me. And proceeded to work my butt off on the practice court. And I learned to volley. I had just been too set in my ways, satisfied with how well I was doing just playing. Allen saw that if I were going to get to another level, I had to change, even if it meant shaking up my game a bit.

I went to that next level, thanks to Foxy. And there were times on the tour, five or six years down the road, when I'd find myself in a painful spot, having just lost an important match, and suddenly I'd hear Allen's laugh in my head. *Lighten up*, it said. *Believe in yourself. Yes, you can. Work harder.*

Andy Roddick, I barely have to tell you, had an amazing 2003, culminating with his first Grand Slam victory at the U.S. Open and his year-ending number-1 ranking (up from number 10 at the beginning of the year, the biggest jump ever accomplished in professional tennis). Before we started working together in June, he had a record of 25 matches won and 11 lost, with one title; from there on, he was 47–8, with five titles. Over one stretch, during the summer hard-court circuit, he was 27–1.

What made the difference?

Ah, that's the $64,000 question, right? I mean, if I told you my secret formula, then everyone would know!

Well, the fact is, I've already been telling you my secret formula, all along—the one that Chiv and Allen Fox and Andre taught me, and that I've been slowly teaching myself over the years. And I'll have a lot more to tell you about, but what it all really comes down to, on my end, is a few not-so-mysterious things: Very hard work. Huge amounts of paying attention. Positiveness to the point of unreasonableness. And having someone's backside to the point of cheerfully doing anything, no matter how (seemingly) small, that makes him feel taken care of.

On the player's end, there's also a lot of hard work, of course. *And* paying attention. And putting up with my unreasonable positiveness. And then there's that final necessity, God-given talent. Otherwise we'd all go out and do it ourselves, right?

The winning coach-player formula simultaneously is both not so mysterious and highly mysterious because it hinges so intricately on the fit between two personalities. Something about Andre and me just clicked. And now, I was discovering (as I had strongly suspected beforehand), Andy and I were clicking, too. There were similarities between the two relationships, but there were also a lot of big differences.

And where the differences were concerned, I had to do a lot of paying attention.

Some coaches, in tennis and other sports too, have a formula. It worked for one, they reason, therefore it will work for another: It *will* work. Will, meaning willpower, is what it's all about for them. And for these guys, invariably, it's "my way or the highway." Plenty of intensity there, but not a lot of flexibility. (And in my mind, a quick road to coach burnout.)

I have a different idea. Yes, there are some basic concepts that I believe in—scouting opponents; hard work; punctuality; courtesy—and if you want to call that a formula, fine. But the cornerstone of my philosophy is something a little less hard-edged: communication.

To me, the most important part of coaching is being able to look through the other person's eyes. I quickly learned with Andre that it didn't matter to him what I or any other player would do in a given situation. Andre was Andre. There were lessons I had to impart to him, but the best way for us to really take it to the next level was for me to watch and listen before piping up myself.

Likewise, the quickest way for me to mess up my new relationship with Andy would have been for me to assume that since I'd learned so much working with Andre, I shouldn't change a thing.

For some coaches, that might've been an easy assumption to make. After all, while Andre and I had almost been contemporaries, only eight and a half years apart in age, I was *twenty-one years* older than Andy—old enough (biologically, anyway) to be his dad. Shouldn't I give him the benefit of my paternal wisdom?

Andy set the tone right away. His wicked sense of humor wouldn't let him take anybody—himself or me—too seriously. The moment I started acting like the Wise Old

Man of Tennis, he let me know it. When we started traveling together, I couldn't help reminiscing about my time
on the tour. I had so much knowledge to pass along!
"Back in the day," I would say. Or, "When I won here in
'87. . . ."

Andy was polite, up to a point. Then he let me know
that enough was enough. "Brad," he said, "I don't *want* to
hear how you won here in 1987. *Everything* with you is
'back in the day.' I'll bet you a dinner in any restaurant
you want that you can't go forty-eight hours without saying 'back in the day' once."

Zing! After I pulled the spear out of my side, I literally
had to put a note to myself on the inside of my hotel-
room door: DO NOT SAY "BACK IN THE DAY!!!"

A short sidebar on paternal wisdom.

My own son, Zach, fifteen years old at the time I write
this, is a fine high-school tennis player. This is—I can't
help it!—a very exciting thing for me.

It is also a very difficult thing for me.

Zach is a lefty, which is only the beginning of how different he is from his old man. He is his mother's son as
well as his father's son: He is artistic, sensitive, thoughtful.
He reads widely; he works very hard in school. When I was
Zach's age, I was burning up the Northern California
junior-tennis circuit—or at least trying to. Academics were

the last thing on my mind. I was totally (and more unreasonably than I knew) dedicated to the idea of becoming a professional tennis player.

Zach isn't me. And wherever he takes his tennis is fine with me. But as a coach and a dad, I can't help getting involved—which quickly leads to getting overinvolved. When I see that Zach's footwork or service toss need work, I can't help talking to him about it, in some detail. I have, as you might imagine, a great deal to say about footwork and the mechanics of the service toss.

Zach doesn't want to hear any of it. He likes hitting tennis balls with me; he'd just like me to keep my lips zipped while I hit. (An unlikely event.)

He's fifteen, an age at which a boy knows his father knows nothing—even if he realizes, deep down, how much his dad really does know. After all, I'm Mr. Famous Tennis Coach. And while it can be fun and exciting to have me as a dad—Zach's gotten to go places, see things, and meet people that a lot of fifteen-year-olds would be envious of—it can also, sometimes, be a giant pain in the ass.

When I go to his matches, for example. There's an ironclad rule in professional tennis that no coaching is allowed during play. It's a rule I happen to think could use some modification, but I abide by it strictly. I have to: I'm a very high-visibility guy out there in my floppy Metallica hat and wraparound shades. The TV cameras are on me all the time. One little third-base-coach-style signal to my guy on court, and I could be in a world of trouble. (And believe me, a few of the less-visible coaches aren't always so scrupulous.)

Now, there's a similar no-coaching rule in high-school matches, and it very definitely extends to parents. But I'm here to tell you, right here and now, that the one and only time in my life I ever got the hook—got ejected from the stands at a tennis match—was at one of Zach's tournaments.

I couldn't help it! (I thought.) Zach happened to be playing this kid whose forehand was weaker than his backhand—I could see it plain as day, but Zach kept hitting to the kid's backhand anyway, and the kid was killing him on that side.

So I made a few gestures. All right, more than a few. I was swinging my hand, nodding my head—doing everything I could to try to mime my very important message: *Hit it to his forehand, damn it!*

The roving lady umpire spotted me (it wasn't hard). "Mr. Gilbert, you should know better," she said. "That's coaching—you have to leave." Out to the parking lot I went. Pretty humiliating, for father and son.

Not to mention ineffective. Zach told me after the match that he'd had no idea why I was acting so weird in the stands! (Maybe he thought it was some especially embarrassing new type of parental cheerleading.)

I'm trying to improve. But when it comes to coaching—or in this case not coaching—my own son, I'm still struggling to figure it all out.

Maybe (I hope not) *paternal wisdom* truly is a contradiction in terms where I'm concerned. Or maybe (I hope) the wisdom I'm just beginning to learn has more to do with shutting up and paying attention than with imparting gems of knowledge.

With Andy, there's definitely been a learning curve. The good news is that we hit it off right away: The chemistry was there. One big thing Andy and Andre have in common with each other (and with me) is that they're both gregarious. They (and I) like to get out and have fun, see people. I could work with someone who didn't like to go out, who preferred keeping to himself, but it would be harder for me.

But any relationship is complicated, even after you think you've scoped out all the angles. Andy and I had great mutual respect, which helped us from the get-go. I might have been twenty-one years older, but I wasn't his dad—he already had a dad—and I wasn't his older brother. He already had one of those, too. I was his coach. I was there to provide a service, in the highest sense of the word. There's a humility to it, and I've come to understand the power that humility can have, in the same way that I understand the weakness of arrogance. What are good manners but a form of humility?

A form of humility that also conveys strength of character.

Early on in my work with Andre, I began calling him boss—and I did the same thing when I started coaching Andy. Andy likes it, not because it makes him feel superior to me, but because it makes him feel taken care of—I have his back.

But the new boss is definitely a different man from the old boss. For one thing, Andy is the messiest guy I've ever met—and that's saying something. I'm not exactly a neat freak when I'm on the road. Andre was. In fact, I would go so far as to say that Andre Agassi is the cleanest person I've ever encountered. He does amazing laundry—he travels with his own fabric softener. He irons his own jeans. Sometimes when we were traveling together, he'd get so upset at the state of my clothes that he would take my laundry and do it for me.

This is not Mr. Roddick. Any hotel room where Andy's staying is a tornado trail of clothing, CDs, and athletic equipment. Any match that Andy's playing is a potential drama, before he even steps on the court: I can't tell you the number of times he's forgotten his ankle braces, or even his shoes. Shoes! Once, just before his night match at a tournament in Basel, Andy told me, smiling, that he'd remembered to bring his braces this time—but that he

had two left tennis shoes in his bag. This was twenty minutes before an 8 P.M. match, and it was ten minutes each
way to the hotel.

I guess I was looking worried. Then I smiled.

"Hey, Andy—K.I.T.," I said.

"K.I.T.?" Andy asked.

I explained. One of my favorite films is *Bowfinger*, star-
ring Steve Martin as a sleazy producer and Eddie Murphy
as Kit Ramsey, a nervous action-picture star whose mantra
(after the letters of his first name) is "Keep it together"—
K.I.T. In a funny-serious way, K.I.T. kind of became our
mantra too, something we'd say with a smile whenever
things got tough.

This was definitely a K.I.T. moment. I got in a car with a
nice lady from tournament transportation, and she proceeded to gun it, James Bond-style, through the narrow
streets of Basel. Halfway to the hotel we hit a traffic jam.

"Do you know a shortcut?" I asked her.

She nodded, screeched into a U-turn, and veered down
a narrow alley. We were flying down this alley, and all of a
sudden there was a car stopped in front of us, waiting for
a parking spot. So I told the nice lady to drive up onto the
sidewalk. She did. But as we passed the stopped car, a guy
started banging on the window, saying that we'd almost
hit someone on the sidewalk. And the guy and his girlfriend were on bikes, and the guy's bike was parked di-
rectly in front of us.

I stepped out of the car and chucked his bike as far as I could. Sometimes you gotta do what you gotta do.

I was back at the tournament at 7:57 P.M., handing Andy his shoes. And, cool as a cucumber, he put the shoes on and walked out onto the court and beat Olivier Rochus of Belgium, 6–4, 6–4.

Just another day at the office for player and coach.

Andy definitely put a few more gray hairs on my head that night. Come to think of it, maybe he's responsible for all of them. He isn't a retiring personality by any stretch. After that first practice, the one where I told him to lose the orange visor, he gave me a shot right back. "I can't believe how eighties your taste in music is," he said, picking up one of my Steve Miller CDs and making a face. "Or is this seventies? Brad, you've got to open up a little bit. Try some new things."

I soon found out just how new he meant.

I've told you that Chiv was my main coaching guru, the Yoda I'd think about in any given situation, but there was one idea I came up with all by myself, and it started with Andre. Sometimes, when I'd be giving him a scouting report at dinner, or gracing him with some other words of wisdom before a match, he'd give me a look that said, *Yeah, it's easy for you to do all the talking—I'm the one who has to play the damn match.*

That was when I first came up with the idea of the Bet.

The first time I lost, I had to shave my head. The next time, I had to shave my chest. Then I had to get an earring. (I'm *really* not an earring guy.) But the last time was sheer inspiration.

Andre won the Australian Open in January 2000, but after that, he was so upset by the simultaneous illnesses of his mother and sister that he had a less than stellar year. He was really struggling with the whole idea of playing tennis. Then things began to look a bit better for his mom and Tammy, and Andre felt better, too. When we got back to Melbourne at the beginning of 2001, he said to me, "What are you going to do if I win this tournament? You've got to do something good."

We were driving to the courts. And all at once I said, "You know what, dude? As soon as you win this tournament, literally the first thing I'm going to do is this. We're going to get in the car, leave the facility, turn the corner, and I'm going to go right over to the Yarra River"—that's this fairly disgusting, polluted river that snakes through Melbourne—"and I'm going swan-dive in, fully clothed, and go for a swim."

A.A. smiled. "I like it. I like it," he said. And I liked that he liked it. I knew that in every match he played at the Australian that year, he would have that little germ of an idea in his head—he was going to get me, Mr. Germ-o-Phobe, to swan-dive into the filthy Yarra.

It worked. Andre won his second title there in two years. And it all happened exactly the way I said it would—we got in the car after the ceremony, Gil in the front with Peter the driver, A.A. and I in the back, nobody saying a word. We turned the corner. Nobody said a word. Peter drove right over to the promenade by the Yarra and stopped the car. I got out—and Andre got out with me. I took a running dive, screaming, "Geronimo!"—and Andre dove in with me. Gil and Peter were just staring at us, laughing their heads off.

When we got back to the hotel, everybody was lined up, ready to congratulate Andre, and in we walked, covered in mud, feet squishing, looking like Creatures from the Black Lagoon. Yay, team!

You could have told me before I started working with Andy that coaching a new guy would be similar but very different, and I would've nodded, but I wouldn't have truly understood until I got to know the new guy. My gut instinct about hitting it off with Andy proved to be right, and that was essential, but there were surprises every day. The differences from Andre went way beyond messiness versus neatness. One of Andy's favorite hobbies was skydiving—something Andre wouldn't do in a million years. Something *I* wouldn't do in a million years. Whenever Andy told me how much he loved it, I'd say, "I just would never do that; it sounds pathetic to me."

Yet another instance where I should have kept my mouth shut.

As Andy and I motored through his incredible hard-court summer of 2003, two Tennis Masters Series tournaments, Montreal and Cincinnati, loomed on the horizon. The Tennis Masters Series, aka TMS or Super 9, is a group of nine events that all the top 10 players on the tour must play. Andy had never won a Super 9 tournament. Now, I thought, was his time.

And so I decided to offer a friendly wager.

I told him about the bets I'd made with Andre—Andy shook his head. Kid stuff. He smiled in a dangerous way and said, "What would be your worst fear?"

I answered without thinking. "Jumping out of a plane, man," I said.

"Okay," Andy said. "If I win Canada, you've got to jump out of a plane."

"Okay, boss," I said. "You got it."

I'd said it, but did I really mean it? I had to mean it. I couldn't even imagine going up in a plane with a parachute on my back, let alone jumping out, but I'd made a commitment.

And part of what this was about was taking some of the pressure off. Getting Andy away from thinking, *I've got to win,* and into thinking, *I've got to make frickin' B.G. jump out of a plane, because it's the last thing he ever wants to do.*

But what it was mostly about was breaking out of the

box. After all, could Andy imagine winning a Super 9? If he could take that one big step, the idea of taking the next one—winning a Slam—would seem that much less impossible. If he could make his leap, I could make mine. Well, not *could*. *Could* didn't even seem like part of the equation for me. *Would have to* was more to the point.

One thing was certain: As far as I was concerned, Andy definitely had the better side of the bet.

After every round he won, he'd say, "We're going to jump out of a plane." And I would say, "Win another round, and we'll see." He kept winning. Especially thrilling was his semifinal win against Roger Federer, who had a record of 4–0 on him, including the Wimbledon semifinal that year. Their match in Montreal was incredibly tight and competitive—each player won the exact same number of games, and in the end, the victory came down to four points in the final tiebreaker. In the final, Andy cruised against Argentina's David Nalbandian, a player most people don't cruise against.

I wish he'd savored his victory a little more. As soon as he came into the locker room with the winner's cup, it wasn't, "I've just won my first Super 9," it was, "When are we going skydiving?"

I felt like echoing that famous New Yorker cartoon: "How's never? Is never good for you?"

But a bet is a bet. And they don't mean much unless you pay off right away.

And this one was really going to cost me.

I'm a little bit prone to motion sickness. All right, I'm a lot prone to it. If I sit backwards on a train, I get nauseous immediately. Boats are no good. Forget roller coasters. So the idea of skydiving didn't even compute.

Yet nine days after the Montreal final—in the interim, Andy also won the Super 9 in Cincinnati; during which I forbade him to jump (he thought I was just stalling)—I found myself with Andy in New Jersey, putting on this incredibly uncomfortable parachute rig and doubting my sanity. Andy just kept laughing at me. It was around 97 degrees that August afternoon, but as I stepped into the fifty-year-old crop-dusting plane, I felt numb.

There were ten of us on this plane. Nine maniacs and one numb neurotic Jew. I was supposed to jump in tandem with this big guy, around six three and 220, and all covered with tattoos. I have to tell you, he wasn't a consoling sight.

Neither was Andy, who kept shouting, over the engine noise, things like, "Nervous, B.G.?"

"I've just got to pay my debt," I kept repeating.

We reached the jump zone. And one by one, Andy and the other seven jumped out of the plane, till finally it was just Tattoo Guy and me.

Then we hit an air pocket.

"Getting choppy! We've got to turn around!" the pilot yelled.

But suddenly I had a vision of Andy plaguing me for the rest of my days about wussing out. "We've got to do this!" I yelled back.

So the pilot circled around again, and the air had calmed down. Tattoo Man and I, tethered together, stepped to the doorway. It was cooler up at 13,500 feet, but in my jumpsuit and parachute rig, I was totally soaked with sweat. It was pouring out of me. I was just getting up the courage to look out the doorway when Mr. Tattoo yelled "Geronimo!"—shades of the Yarra River—and out I went with him, and there was nothing between me and the New Jersey real estate below but two and a half miles of summer air.

It took us a minute and fifteen seconds to free-fall from 13,500 feet down to 5,000—a minute and a quarter, and about fifty revolutions. Round and round we went. Then my jump partner pulled the rip cord, and we jerked back up around a hundred feet as our chute opened. *Okay, we're going to make it*, I thought. *It's okay now.*

Little did I know that the last 5,000 feet would be the worst experience I'd ever had.

My partner was navigating us back and forth, back and forth, trying to steer us toward the drop zone and see a little scenery at the same time. And I started getting so motion sick that I couldn't even talk. My jaws locked, otherwise I would have yelled, "Stop navigating!"

Then we landed. I was fine with that part. The earth felt

good. Then someone was pointing a video camera in my face and asking, "Would you ever do it again?"

"Ah, I don't know," I said. "I've got to think about it."

"How are you feeling?" Mr. Videocam asked.

"Okay" was the word that came out of me, though I wouldn't say it exactly corresponded to the way I felt. I lay on the ground for around twenty minutes, soaked with sweat, my skin dead white. Andy found all this fairly humorous.

We got in the car and started to head back to New York. But after around fifteen seconds, I said, "Pull over."

My cell phone rang while I was in the bushes across the road. I'd left the phone sitting on the seat of the car. Andy answered. It was Kim calling.

"Who's this?" she asked.

"This is Andy," Andy said.

"Where's Brad?" Kim asked.

"Oh, Brad's across the road, parking some green shine in someone's yard," Andy said.

And thus a great partnership was cemented.

> The vast majority of people go through life by routine. Think about it. Pay attention! Wake up!

I have to confess, my wife was not thrilled about my experiment in skydiving. (That's an understatement.) I also have to say that I'm not in a hurry to do it again. (Never would be good for me.) But paying off on my bet to Andy wasn't a macho thing—it was a totally serious way of showing him that if he could go the distance, so could I. The experience made us closer as a team, and showed us we really could climb to new heights, and even jump from them. (Within a month of our touching down in that New Jersey field, Andy would become the youngest American number 1 ever.)

But I also have to tell you that as scared as I was, as sick as I got, something in me was totally ready for the experience. I'd been through plenty of tough times before in my time on the tour (all right, all right, *back in the day*— Andy, I owe you a dinner). Especially in my rookie years, when it really was sink or swim.

I always say you don't necessarily have to have been a good player to be a good coach. But having been a good player doesn't mean you can't coach well—especially if you really understand what battling through adversity is all about.

6. You Cannot Be Negative

"Negativity is like the common cold. You can catch it in a minute."

—*Tom Chivington*

"Get over it! If you lost Tuesday, and you're still talking about it Friday, what are you going to do when Monday rolls around?"

—*B.G.*

A couple of years ago, John McEnroe published a book—you may remember it—called *You Cannot Be Serious*. In the book, I was very flattered to see a rather lengthy discussion of our match at the year-ending 1985 Masters tournament in New York's Madison Square Garden, a match in which I beat John for the only time in my career (against 13 losses). The event apparently loomed (maybe even still looms) large in John's mind. For one thing, it seems to have sent him off the tour and into temporary retirement for a good deal of 1986. He wrote, "I looked up to the heavens and thought, 'Someone is telling me something here. Because if I can lose to Brad Gilbert, something is seriously wrong. I've got to take a look at myself. I've got to reevaluate not only my career but my life.' "

Now, since this was essentially the same thing he told the press right after that match, it didn't sting much to read it sixteen years later. But there was another thing John wrote that got me thinking a little bit:

What was it about him? It mostly boiled down to this: I've never seen anybody as negative on a tennis court. Eeyore had nothing on Brad—he had a black cloud over his head from the moment he walked out there, and he never seemed satisfied until he got you feeling pretty gloomy, too. It almost seemed to be his game plan. He'd look like he was going to commit hara-kiri in the warm-up. Then he did a running commentary while he played, berating himself on every single point (as if people cared), and justifying every mistake he made: "I can't believe I hit that backhand down the line instead of crosscourt. Why didn't I hit that drop volley there? Why didn't I hit my first serve wide instead of going up the middle?"

As an opponent, you'd hear everything he said, because he'd say it loud enough for the people in the stands to catch every word. And it would get under your skin and infect you.

I'm sure Gilbert won a lot of matches by bending the emotional rules. Some people just feed off negativity. I think that for a long time—no surprise—that was something I did myself.

For a long time! Anybody who's seen John play lately, in exhibitions or on the senior circuit—where he usually gives a vintage performance, in every sense—might wonder exactly how long a time he meant.

But I'm not here to go off on John. We all have our own

path to walk, and the fact is that I haven't always been such an angelic character myself. There was some truth in what he wrote about me—as I admitted, years before, in my book, *Winning Ugly*. On a bad day on the tour, I was all too capable of getting down on myself in a very public way, giving just the kind of negative running commentary that John mentioned.

Yet since he really only saw me on a court when he was playing me (John never felt he had to scout anybody), he missed one crucial fact: I mainly acted like that when I was up against somebody who had my number. There weren't too many on the tour who did. But clearly, John had my number big time.

John had almost everybody's number, because he was a genius, one of the greats of tennis history. The first time I ever played him, in the third round at Wimbledon in 1983, it was like going down in an elevator that didn't stop at the floors—whoosh!—it happened so *fast*. It was usually the same way with Ivan Lendl, another great. With those guys, if you were just playing decently and they were on their game, they would kick your butt something fierce—and they could do it very quickly. It wasn't slow and methodical.

The pro tour was a great way of making a living. I had no complaints then; I have none now. But the tour was anything but a love fest. So how did I get to be Mr. Positive?

Well, for one thing, most of the time I wasn't playing

McEnroe and Lendl. In my early days as a pro, at the beginning of the eighties, I was up against guys who, like me, were just getting started. All of them were really fine players who, for one reason or another, never came close to becoming household names, for one reason: They didn't stick around.

The fact that I did stick around not only says something about my tennis skills but it also says a lot about who I am and where I came from.

The truth is that negativity has always been skin deep with me—maybe because I resisted it from the get-go. I had to. When I started out in professional tennis, there was so much negativity around, it was ridiculous.

In the fall of 1981, I took a semester off from school to get a little taste of the pro tour, and to try to get on the rankings map. I had a little bankroll from scalping Oakland Raiders tickets—yes, I was quite the junior entrepreneur—so I could pay for my own airfare. I was ready to take on the world.

But you couldn't just jump straight onto the big events on the tour—you had to build up enough pro points. At the beginning, I had to try to qualify for lesser tournaments. Back then, there was a kind of Asian minitour in November and December, with events in Hawaii, the Philippines, Taiwan, Japan, and Thailand. Taipei is the one that really stands out in my memory—for all the wrong reasons.

It was an indoor tournament, and the main venue had exactly one court. Qualifying rounds were not high on the list of the tournament organizers' priorities. The qualies had to be held elsewhere, and elsewhere in this case was a little college out in the Taiwanese boonies, where the tennis courts hadn't been resurfaced in so long that they were shiny. There were thirty-two of us fighting it out for four spots in the main tournament. Three rounds: Thirty-two players down to four. Survival-of-the-fittest time.

We all stayed in two dorm rooms at this dinky college—eight bunk beds in each room, like the county lock-up. I almost had a heart attack when I had to go to the bathroom, and I opened the door and saw the toilet—a hole in the floor. Forget about laundry facilities, or transportation back to town. We were all used to living better in the States—and we'd all been taken care of a lot better in college.

It was a six-week grind out there in Southeast Asia, at holiday time. This was long before e-mail or cell phones; an international call was a big deal. It was isolating. Suddenly you really had to be resilient, and a lot of the guys struggled. They missed their girlfriends. They missed this; they missed that. Guys would start bitching. Loudly. "This sucks. Everything sucks." They'd make excuses for why they were losing. The tournament director (or somebody) was screwing them.

But Chiv had given me some advice before I left, and I thought of it now. When guys are hanging out, and everybody's being negative, he'd told me, just go somewhere else. "Negativity is like the common cold," Chiv said. "You can catch it in a minute."

The guys who didn't want to be there in the first place would find excuses to lose. They'd go out drinking and having fun till all hours, and come back feeling so lousy that they couldn't possibly play well. I wasn't charmed to be there, but I knew *why* I was there. I felt the meter was running. I kept it together, and made it through all three rounds, into the main draw.

Where things barely got better.

Since the whole tournament was played on this one indoor court, if you wanted to practice on that surface—it was lightning-fast carpet, and believe me, you needed to practice—you had to get up at five in the morning, ahead of everyone else, to get a half-hour hit in.

And at five A.M., I felt like death warmed over. Although I was now in a hotel instead of college-dorm barracks, my room didn't even have a TV. The bed was so bad, I had to pull the mattress off in the middle of the night and put it on the floor, which the management was none too thrilled about. I hung in there.

I won a round there, and in Manila I qualified and got to the quarterfinals. I was number 220 in the world. *If I start playing full-time*, I thought, *I'll move right up.*

. . .

In 1981, when I was playing tournaments but wasn't yet a pro, I would qualify for some events, and get bounced out of others. When I officially joined the tour, after I left Pepperdine in the spring of 1982, something in my mind shifted. In those days, if you lost in the qualifiers, you got zero—no money, no points. And I thought: *This is for real. I swear to God I'm not going to lose. I'm not going to go somewhere and not get any points and not get any money. It's not going to happen.*

And it didn't. In 1982, I qualified for eight straight tournaments—won twenty-four straight qualifying rounds. It's a record which, I believe, has never been equaled, and one I'm very proud of.

It was also a record that stood me in good stead once I got to the main draws of those tournaments. I had momentum. I had confidence.

And, often as not, I would get beaten.

That's what it's like your first year on the tour. It's rough out there. Lots of strong, seasoned players. Sometimes you lose to people who are better than you are, and sometimes to people who aren't. You have to learn to roll with it. A lot of guys didn't learn. They'd have a bad loss and smash all their racquets in the locker room. (Those were still the days of wooden racquets. I tried to limit my racquet-smashing to one at a time, and in the privacy of my hotel room.) They'd think, *I was a star in college. Why am I struggling out here?*

A case in point: The player will go nameless here. This guy was a college star, and hooked up as a doubles team with a much higher-ranked player. The two of them had some good success and, fueled by that, the guy did pretty well in singles, too, rising as high as number 40 in the world.

But back in those days, you had to defend your points. If you had a good result at a tournament, those points would fall off your record one year later to the day, and if you hadn't replaced that good result with another one, your ranking could drop, fast, and you'd have to play qualifiers again. It made for a lot of pressure if you were on a losing streak: You might find yourself at a tournament with one week, one chance, to defend your points. A lot of players wilted under that heat.

That was exactly what happened to the guy I'm talking about. His ranking dropped, and all at once, he found himself back in the qualies, and he hated it. Beneath his dignity. He'd had that sniff of the big time, and felt he deserved to stay there, no matter what kind of tennis he played. Remember that story I told you earlier about Andre playing Burbank and Vegas in 1997? It was medicine that he needed at the time, and he took it like a man. This other guy was still a spoiled boy when I ran into him, he on his way down and I on my way up. After 1982, I never saw him again.

And after my hardworking year in 1982, I never had to play another qualifier again.

P.S.: I won my first professional tournament in November 1982—at Taipei. One court, lightning-fast carpet. No practice time. Lousy hotel. Something about all of it agreed with me.

I was 21, I was new on the tour, and I won a few, lost a few. My win-loss percentage hovered at around .500. I got hammered sometimes. Now, I didn't like losing any more than the next guy. I could get pretty dramatic about it— temporarily. Failure isn't fun! But losing never set in deep with me. Unlike some players—even some great players— I didn't feel like a loser in life if I lost a match. I didn't want to bring everyone around me down. I always felt: *Thick skin, learn from it, move on. Have a couple of beers, practice tomorrow. I'll get another shot at him down the road.*

That's still a key to my coaching today. I call it short-term memory loss: In other words, Get over it! If you lost Tuesday, and you're still talking about it Friday, what are you going to do when Monday rolls around?

When I was at Pepperdine, I used to practice with a guy who was already on the tour, Brian Teacher. Teach was about seven years older than me, a tall guy who'd boom every serve, cruise in to net, and smash a winner. The year before I met him, he'd been number 12 in the world. He could play.

Teach used to just crush me, every time out. For about three months in early 1982, we practiced twice a week, best of three sets, except that it never went to three. The scores were always 6–1, 6–2, or 6–3, 6–1. He had a long face, long arms and legs: I thought of him as the Praying Mantis. Deadly. Especially to me.

Most guys, if they're beating you that badly, will try to find someone more on their own level. Teach was a super-nice guy, though, and he must've gotten something out of our practices, because no matter what the score was, he'd always say, "When do you want to play again?"

The first time I came up against him on the tour, I immediately flashed back to all those practices. *Oh, man,* I thought. *I'm playing the Praying Mantis.* Well, there's nothing like the power of negative thinking: Teach crushed me, 6–4, 6–0. (Even more amazing, the match was on clay, which wasn't Teach's best surface. Instead of thinking about that, though—instead of thinking at all—I mentally conceded him the match before it began. A huge mistake on my part.)

I only played him one more time after that, and I finally beat him. It was the finals at Livingston, New Jersey, in 1985. It took me three years, but I got Teach! Even in practicing with him, I don't think I ever won a set until that match. At that point in my career, I was ranked a lot higher than he was, and he was on his way down—but he still had that mental mojo over me.

I struggled with it. Even after I won the first set, even when I pulled ahead 5–4 in the second, and he was serving to stay in the match, I was still worried. But when I got out of my chair on the changeover, he couldn't even stand up. His face was white. It was the end of July, 95 degrees.

When he finally stood up, he could barely move. I closed out the match in straight sets, but Teach gave me a hard time about it afterwards: "See, the first time you beat me is because I get heatstroke!"

Teach was one of the few older players who were nice to me when I first came on the tour. Two others were Tom Gullikson and Vince Van Patten. They were in the minority. The rest just felt too threatened by a young up-and-comer. "Rook," they'd call you—short for "rookie." I remember one time at a tournament in Washington, D.C., I'd won a round on a blistering hot day, and I was lying on the floor of the locker room afterward (it was in a house trailer—very glamorous!), so tired I couldn't move, with my gear lying all around me. And this tour veteran struts in and looks at me like I'm garbage. "Hey, rook," he says. "Move your goddamn stuff."

It was tough out there week to week: You were far away from home, and if you woke up at two in the morning someplace in Europe or Asia—the way I often did—there was no CNN, no Internet, no *USA Today*. Sometimes I'd just pace back and forth in my hotel room, or swing my racquet. I swung my racquet a lot.

It was pretty lonely, but it made you tougher. Those were the times that you had to be tough to push through. A lot of guys who turned pro in my era left fairly early—they'd had too many of those nights. Some of these guys had been terrific juniors and college players.

There was one guy who I thought would've done much better. An All-American in college, a huge guy, with an overpowering serve. He beat me in the 1982 U.S. Open, serving something like forty-two aces. He just blew me off the court—I could practically feel my little wood racquet shaking whenever he was serving.

Two years later, I played him at an indoor tournament, and I was totally intimidated—the fast surface favored his big game. I beat him 6–1, 6–1. He was like a shadow of himself. And then he pretty much fell off the tour.

It wasn't the other players who beat this guy. It was the tour itself.

> How is it possible to be competitive and not lose your love for the game? That's a real question.

Everyone knows what it feels like to lose a battle—in sports, in business, in life. But what do you do when an adversary, or maybe just life, really stops you in your tracks? When, even while part of you feels the situation is temporary, another part of you is afraid you might not be able to go on?

I've run into the wall in both my playing and coaching careers, and it's rough. The definition of where you are is that you can't see beyond it. If it's my player who's stalled, I'm there to help him, and even though it's hard work, we always find a way through.

But on the couple of occasions when it was just me (once before I met Chiv, and once when he wasn't traveling with me yet), I had to figure it out for myself. The solution I hit on was to reach far back to basics, in a way that had some of my fellow players scratching their heads.

The solution I hit on (sorry about the pun) was the wall itself.

7. Hitting the Wall

The most important opponent you will ever have to face is yourself.

"I was thinking, *I don't know if I want to do it anymore.*"

—B.G.

When I told you about my first tournament win, at Taipei in 1982, I left out the best part: I won that final on one foot.

There's a story behind it, a story of pure momentum. In September of that year, I played my last qualifier ever, at San Francisco. And even though I lost in the first round of the main draw, I'd now built up enough points to be number 100 in the world. That was when I decided to try the Asian tour again.

There were no superstars in those events, nobody in the top 20; just a lot of guys ranked 30, 40, 50. When I hit 100, I thought, *If I play lights-out tennis, I can break into the top 50 by the end of the year.* And as soon as I hit the first tournament on my Pacific swing, in sunny Hawaii, it looked like I was on my way.

The year before at that event, as an amateur testing out the tour, I'd qualified and made it to the quarters, beating the number 1 seed, Harold Solomon, in the process. That was a major win for me, and now, this year, I had a lot of points to defend in Hawaii.

I did even better this time around, making it to the semis. And from there on, I went on a pretty good streak. I got a special exempt into the Sydney Indoor, a major tournament, where I beat Vitas Gerulaitis, number 4 in the world, in the first round, and made it to the quarters. I made it to the round of 16 in the Japan Open. My ranking was climbing; I had a straight shot. I would play Taipei and Bangkok, and then, since I had the points for it, I would head for the big time: the Australian Open.

Taipei was early November. I cruised through to the finals, beating three top seeds along the way, and then came up against Craig Wittus. Now, Craig was a hell of a nice guy, but at around 160 in the world, he was having the tournament of his career. He had made it to the finals as a qualifier! He was hot as a pistol, but I had just come off beating number 4 in the world. Frankly, Craig Wittus was a dream draw for me.

And the match began to play out just that way. I was at the top of my game in the first set, serving at 5–1, 30–love, when I came in to net on an approach shot. Wittus hit a lob up to my backhand side, not much of a lob, really. . . . I decided I didn't even have to run around the backhand overhead to hit a winner. So I backhanded it—and came down the wrong way on my left foot. The foot completely bent under, and I collapsed in agony.

While I was rolling on the ground in pain, Wittus came over and looked down at me. "Man, you'd better get up," he said. "You're playing too well for me to just get a lucky win here." I couldn't believe he said that! Out came Bill Norris, the trainer. Bill, who's now the ATP's senior trainer, is a hell of a nice guy, who, with his straight blond hair and granny glasses, happens to look exactly like the late John Denver. Still—here's my twisted logic—I've always called Bill "Chuck," after *Chuck* Norris. Get it? Anyway, Bill helped me to the sideline and looked at the ankle. "I think you sprained it, Brad," he said.

"Chuckie, just tape me up, buddy," I said.

"I don't know if I'd advise playing on that foot, Brad."

"Just tape me up, Chuckie."

So Bill taped me up. Basically, he made a cast for my left ankle out of tape. Then I put on my sock, and he taped over my sock again—and I'm telling you, on one good ankle, I limped through and won the match, 6–1, 6–4.

A victory that was more like a defeat, as it turned out.

I thought that if I pushed on to Bangkok, the ankle would be okay. The ankle wasn't okay. On the plane over there, it ballooned to three times its normal size. I had to wait four days in Bangkok until the swelling came down enough for me to take a plane back home.

And then I was back home, limping around on crutches

and not in the finest of moods. But I was twenty-one, and resilient—and mainly, I was twenty-one. Every once in a while, I just couldn't help getting a rush of blood. One month later, I felt ready to give the ankle a try.

I was crazy! There was a big tournament in Hartford, Connecticut—a special sixteen-man event which, even as number 50 in the world (I'd made the magic number), I would need to qualify for.

So I entered the qualies—the hell with my bad ankle! (Looking back, I wish I had never done that: I learned much later from Andre that I just wasn't treating my body the way I should've been.) And I won three rounds of qualies and made it into the main draw on sheer adrenaline, because if you lost in the qualies you got zip, whereas if you lost even the first round in the main draw, you got six thousand dollars. And that was one heck of a payday at that time—but I could do even better than that, I thought. I could get past the first round. That's when I found out that my first-round opponent was . . . Ivan Lendl.

Sometimes you draw Wittus; sometimes it's Lendl. This was the first of my 16 losses to Ivan. I came to think of him as my personal Freddy Krueger.

It was all over very quickly. Ivan scorched me, 6–2, 6–2, and to tell the truth, the match wasn't even that close. My foot was really bothering me—that's my excuse. Maybe if the ankle had been perfect, I would've gotten one more game off him.

But now my ankle was really in bad shape. I was off for six weeks, and then I went out to test the waters of 1983.

I should've stayed off the ankle another month. But I was not only young and hot-blooded, I was also anxious. My ranking wasn't exactly rising while I was sitting at home.

Still, I didn't do my ranking any favors by rushing back onto the tour. I had my first really bad stretch over the first three months of 1983, losing to good players, losing to lesser players. The ankle was improving, but my confidence was not.

It was my first crisis as a professional. Now that my physical excuse had expired, what was I doing wrong? It was tempting to lose my temper, smash some racquets. Instead, I tried to understand why I was losing all these matches. Why was I so tight on my second serve? Why wasn't I hitting out on my forehand? Was there a point, before the point when I choked in a tight match, when I was making some mistake I wasn't even aware of? For the first time, I had to take a hard, hard look at every aspect of my game, mental and physical.

It wasn't the first time, though. When I was sixteen, I had a little bit of a burnout as a junior player. Just like with my ankle injury, there was a physical excuse. In this case, it had to do with the fact that I hadn't grown as fast as most of the guys I was playing. Suddenly some of them—including guys I'd defeated when I was younger, but who had sprouted up faster than me—were beating up on me a bit. Meanwhile, various coaches kept telling me I had to change my game. I was struggling.

And I was struggling with my desire to play. My dad was a cheerful, hugely enthusiastic guy, and my biggest motivator when I was a junior. When I was ten years old, he took me to see the Davis Cup semifinal, the U.S. against Romania, in Alamo, California, about an hour from my house. I remember watching the doubles, Stan Smith and Erik Van Dillen against Ilie Nastase and a guy named Ionel Santeiu—an incredible match, which we won. And while we were driving home, Dad said to me, very matter-of-factly, "You'll play Davis Cup."

I believed him. I believed I would be a professional tennis player someday—even when I'd only grown to five foot two by age sixteen. All of a sudden, though, I wasn't so sure. Dad was starting to get concerned. "Who are you playing with?" he'd ask me. "Who are you practicing with?" I felt pestered, persecuted. Ain't adolescence great? And when I didn't give Dad an enthusiastic answer, he would say, "You're not practicing enough; you've got to apply yourself more."

Meanwhile, I was thinking, *I don't know if I want to do it anymore.*

Not that I wanted to give up the game. But suddenly, spending three hours a day on it, every day, felt like a lot.

Suddenly, it felt like a lot to leave the house at five-thirty or six on a Saturday morning to go to some tournament where I'd spend the entire day.

That was when I hit the wall.

Literally. Earlier that year, I'd had the chance to practice a few times with a tour player named Jeff Borowiak at the Berkeley Tennis Club. Boro was a hell of a nice guy and, at number 30 or 40 in the world, the best player by far I had ever hit with at that point. Jeff was also a thoughtful guy, and his coach was professional tennis's greatest eccentric, Torben Ulrich, the Danish hippie (Torben's son Lars, the drummer for Metallica, is my close friend and neighbor today).

Torben was into meditation, and he taught Boro about practicing against the wall. It calmed you down, Torben felt, and got you superfocused. Jeff would even hit volleys against the wall with a one-pound weight on his racquet to strengthen his wrists.

I watched, I learned.

About a mile from my house there was a baseball field, Hampton Field, with a gigantic freestanding concrete wall, maybe 30 feet wide and 20 feet high. I'd take my racquet and a bag of balls and just go play on the wall for an hour. I wouldn't have to deal with some kid getting all competitive or hooking me on line calls. I wouldn't have to listen to anybody telling me to change my game. And most of all, I wouldn't have to listen to, "Who are you playing with? Who are you practicing with?" I'd draw a box on the wall with a piece of chalk, and see how many times in a row I could hit the ball into the box.

It was a beautiful thing to do—not just calming and meditative, but amazingly good for my game. You'd be surprised how hard it is to hit a quickly rebounding tennis ball into a small chalk square ten or twenty times in a row. Forehand, backhand; forehand, backhand. Weird rebound—another backhand! You learn to get your racquet back *fast*. You learn to get the hitches out of your swing.

For some reason, when I look back and remember hitting against the wall, it's always cold out. I gear up in my hooded sweatshirt. Just me and my stick and the ball and the wall. I'd pretend I was playing the number-1 guy from a high school across the county. I'd imagine the rallies, the scores, my terrific crosscourt passing shots. And then I'd get back into my car and feel I'd really made some progress.

I know I actually did. The wall was my Zen. My focus, my purpose. My judge and jury. The wall never missed. That year, when I was sixteen, I think it made me ten times better. And at the end of the day, I could tell my Dad, "Yeah, I practiced with somebody."

Getting my ass kicked by Lendl at the end of 1982 had felt kind of like hitting a wall. And what I learned from the experience was this: When you take a beating, it's not the end of the world. You just have to fight it off. My dad used to say, "You've got to have thick skin." When I lost a match as a kid, sometimes he'd kill me with his positiveness. He might have advice for what I could have done differently, how I could've concentrated better, but he was never negative. "We'll do it next week," he'd say. That's exactly what he told me after the Lendl match: "You'll have another chance to play next week. And you made six thousand bucks—that's incredible."

But staying positive meant more than just having thick skin. Sometimes when I was banging the ball against that wall at Hampton Field, kids on their way to their baseball games would walk past and give me a funny look. "What are you doing, hitting on the wall?" they'd say. "Don't you ever get tired of it?" I never got tired of it—that was peace.

In Taipei my first time, in 1981, when all of us in the qualifiers were stuck out in that college in the boonies, where the conditions were so bad, I found a wall to hit against. And there, too, the other guys would look at me like I had a screw loose. "What are you doing that for?" they'd ask. "You okay?"

"I'm fine," I told them. "Just relaxing my brain a little bit." Maybe that's one thing that happened to a lot of the players who came up with me: When things got tough, they had no place to go inside. They'd moved smoothly from the juniors to college to the pros, and suddenly they weren't doing that well. They'd been used to kicking everybody's ass, and now they were the ones getting their asses kicked. It's tough to be a former star who's now number 150 in the world, having to play qualifiers or losing every week in the first round, just barely hanging on. A lot of guys couldn't handle it. They thought they were better than that, but then they'd get a 6–2, 6–2 ass-kicking, and they'd get demoralized. And they would always have a ton of excuses. "Three weeks ago I got to the quarters in Manila." They would live for months on that one good result, but then, when there were no more good results, they'd get that look in their eyes: I called it Tap City. When I saw that look, I knew they were history.

In my mind, last week was last week. If I had a bad tournament, I would think, *Okay, new 52-week calendar, starting today.* I always felt, after the initial shock: *Hey, I got my ass kicked. All right, let's get back to work. Let's get after it.* The thought that finally settled into my mind after that Lendl match was, *Okay, I've got a long way to go.*

In many ways, 1983 set the pattern for who I was to become as a professional tennis player and a coach. After inching under number 50 in the world toward the end of 1982, I got injured and slipped to number 54. And then in 1983, I had my long bad streak—fighting and struggling every week, losing in the first and second rounds of a lot of tournaments and not winning a single event. Call it second-year blues. At one point, my ranking fell into the eighties. But then, in the last four months of the year, I began winning a little bit. Just a little bit. (One thing that helped was returning to the scene of my first tour win, at Taipei. It was good to be back.)

At the end of 1983, I didn't feel especially good about myself, but on the other hand, I'd battled out of the eighties to get back to number 62, a net loss of only eight slots from the year before.

What I learned during that hard year was that, for better or worse, I was not a tennis player to whom things were going to come easily. I had talent, but if I was going to prevail against other talented players (and more-talented players), I was going to have to summon every bit of knowledge I had about the game, and every inner resource, *and* work my ass off. And take some hits.

I like cars—American cars. That's how I thought of myself : a big old American car. I wound up playing on the men's professional tennis tour for thirteen and a half years—maybe the equivalent of putting 600,000 miles on an actual vehicle. I was in it for the long haul. I would fix a flat tire here, fix another flat there. Change the oil. Get that old car on the freeway and put it on cruise control. Week after week. Year after year.

In 1984, my car began hitting on all cylinders. I'd learned I could get through the hardest times on the tour; I had a little bit of seasoning. And with the bit of confidence I gained at the end of 1983 (and with my little black book getting more and more detailed every week),

I felt I knew my way around professional tennis. I was less intimidated; for the first time I was starting to feel a little more confident about what I was doing. I began losing less in the first and second rounds, making more quarterfinals and semis. I won two tournaments, one in Columbus, Ohio, and then one last time in my beloved Taipei. (After my second win there, they closed the tournament for good.) I rose to number 23 in the world. It wasn't meteoric, but it was steady. *Hey*, I thought. *I'm really a pro.*

A lot of parents come up to me and, knowing what I've done with Andre and Andy, beg me to do my magic on their tennis-playing kids. As I said back at the beginning, there is no magic pill. A.A. knew before I did that I could help him. He found me, for which I'm forever grateful. I happen to have started off with one of the great players of our time. Then I stopped, and then came round two, with a guy who has the potential to be one of the great players of his time. I helped Andre to climb back to the heights he'd reached before (and higher); I'm helping Andy climb to the heights I know he's capable of reaching.

But they both had (and have) it in them.

Maybe I was an overachiever as a player—maybe not. It didn't hurt that I had that 600,000-mile work ethic. (Another statistic I own, that I'm as proud of as I am of my year of batting a thousand in the qualifiers: I finished every match I ever started. No injury, cramps, or illness ever stopped me. My own personal Ripken.) One thing I do know is that, for better or worse, I was sometimes motivated by fear. Even as recently as this year, in an exhibition match against Michael Chang, with Andy watching, my main motivation was really not wanting to embarrass myself out there. I didn't. (I won, 6–4.) A big difference between me and Andre and Andy is that that's something they're never afraid of.

Still, while *Winning Ugly* is a phrase I don't mind having attached to me, I will also confess, as modestly as possible, to some real talent for the game of tennis. I'll never claim I was great. Yet one of the lessons Andre taught me was how he peaked, physically and mentally, for the biggest events he played, especially the Grand Slams. It was a lesson I learned too late to help me as a player. I never consciously peaked; I just gutted it out for week after week, year after year. Fix the flat. Change the oil.

So maybe I could have done a little better. Perhaps I was even a bit of an underachiever. My best Grand Slam results were a quarterfinal each at Wimbledon and the U.S. Open. Maybe I could've reached a semi or two, or even gone on a tear and made a final.

But I know what my level was, and it was different from Andre's and Andy's. And I know that if I started working with a player who was number 60 in the world, I would have to do the greatest coaching job in the history of the world to take him, say, to number 27—and everybody would be surprised and disappointed that I hadn't made him number 3.

You work with what you have.

And it's easy to lose sight of how much work there is, and how long it takes, even at the highest levels. How sometimes, everyone hits the wall.

A story: The first year Andre and I started working together, he didn't exactly shoot right to the top. In fact, the first few months were pretty much of a downer: It just felt as though he couldn't win a close match. In May, at the French Open, he lost 7–5 in the fifth set to Thomas Muster, a very tough player to have drawn in the second round. In June, at Wimbledon, he lost in five sets to Todd Martin in the round of sixteen. Then in July, in Washington, D.C., he lost in the third round to a New Zealander named Brett Steven, 6–4 in the third set. It was a hot, steamy night, and it was a low point for both of us. Andre's head was down. Here was a guy he was way better than, and I can't even say that Andre played that badly, but somehow Brett Steven had magic in him that night. And Andre and I were in some kind of bad little rut.

I remember saying to him, "You've just got to win one close match, and everything is going to click. Because in all these close matches that you're losing, you're just not finding a way to win them, and these other guys are playing big. Somehow, the next time, you've just got to play a little bigger. You've got to go *win it* under pressure, and everything is going to click in."

Both our heads were down a little bit when we arrived in Toronto at the end of July. (This was the same Super 9 tournament that Andy would win, in 2003, to force me to go skydiving. The event moves back and forth every year between Toronto and Montreal.) Fortunately—or actually, somewhat unfortunately—Andre had a bye for the first round, and then blew out Jakob Hlasek, of Switzerland, 6–1, 6–1. A bye followed by a blow-out is good for your energy level, but it doesn't exactly get you into the into-the-trenches mode you need for a big event. And Andre's opponent in the next round was David Wheaton, who had been a bit of a nemesis of his since their days of training together back at Nick Bollettieri's tennis academy in Florida.

Now, I was still playing the tour at this point, and the funny thing about David Wheaton is that I had a 7–0 record against him. The guy had never beaten me! And Andre Agassi, with his God-given gift, had a 2–3 record against Wheaton, and was a little worried about this match. Tennis is a funny game. Players match up all kinds of different ways against each other. (But one amazing thing about A.A., to me, is that he has never, ever, taken anyone for granted. Once I started scouting his opponents, he never let me stop, even if I'd seen a guy play a hundred times before. It was one of the things he did that made a better coach out of me.)

"Andre, you're going to be fine," I told him, about the Wheaton match. "I've never lost to this guy—you're going to be fine." And Andre goes out, and they have this unbelievably brutal match. Wheaton won the first set, 6–3. Andre won the second set, 6–1. And then the deciding set turned into a dogfight.

I was sitting in the stands, sweating . . . I'm joking. Outwardly, I was my usual picture of calm reassurance. *Inside,* I was sweating. I kept thinking, *If he can just pull through here, everything will be fine.* But I could see Andre was a little tentative: He just wasn't playing the way I thought he should be playing on the big points.

The third set went to a tiebreaker. Andre saved two match points. Then Wheaton had match point again, on his serve. And the guy had a big serve. He hit a huge kicker out wide, and Andre made an unbelievable stick save and wound up winning the point, and the next one—and the next one, to win the match.

Man, I was excited! But this was a place I really needed Keep It Together in my game. Think of Chiv. Just go to work on the next match. There were three more rounds to play in this tournament. If Andre had lost, I wouldn't have let the emotion out, either. Some coaches are screamers. There are some very successful screamers. But I believe a culture of fear helps no one. If Andre had lost that squeaker against Wheaton, I would have said something like this: "Let's try to go back to 4–all when you had the two break points. Andre, you played defensive. David went for those shots. Imagine we have those two points to play over right now. Why don't you be the one taking the shots? You have bigger shots than him. Don't let him take the risk before you. You've got better shots." And so the next time he found himself in a similar situation, he'd think about taking a rip.

And if I stood there and screamed at him about losing? I wouldn't be coaching, he wouldn't get anything out of it—we'd just be two people making no gain.

But he didn't lose that match; he won. And the reason I was so excited about it was this: It was the first time I'd ever really seen Andre dig one out. He didn't play incredible tennis overall, but he managed to gut this match out—and when he came off the court, he was shaking his head.

I knew that reaction. I knew his mind-set: A.A. didn't like to win a match that way. He thought he should play perfect tennis every time; and if he didn't, he should lose. The gods think differently from us mere mortals.

But in this case, I felt I had to change his thinking. This match felt like a watershed, both in his career and in our new player-coach relationship. I said, "Dude, this is what everything is about. If you can win a match playing at 60 percent of where you feel your game really is, but you're

100 percent mentally, that's way better than if you're hitting the ball like a dream, but you're only 60 percent there mentally."

He looked interested—tentatively.

I said, "You know what? You just battered through this thing. Now you have an opportunity to play another day. You're still in it. Now let your game thrive."

And you know what? In the next round, he had a match against Sergi Bruguera that was just as brutal—and that he was just as lucky to get out of. But it was as if a light switch had gone on in his mind: *I can win these matches.* He was shaking his head a little less after this one.

Andre went on to win blow-outs in the semifinals and finals, scoring his first tournament victory since February. I could read his mind through his broad smile: *I'm back,* he was thinking.

Four weeks later, he won his first U.S. Open.

Everybody likes a blow-out win. Everybody except me. I like the tough match you gut out and win, the one that normally would have sent you home. Sometimes, if you're a perfectionist, you can drive yourself into the ground. The old Andre would've been angry at himself for playing badly in the Wheaton and Bruguera matches. And if he'd stayed angry, maybe he would have lost the next match, because his attitude wasn't positive.

The spin I like to put onto blow-out victories is this: *It's the match that you dug out that gave you that chance.*

Sometimes you have to hit against the wall. Sometimes you have to punch through it.

> Confidence flows all too easily into complacency.

"If it ain't broke, don't fix it," people say.

I don't necessarily agree.

Another way of interpreting that sentence is: Success is nice. When you have it, don't monkey with it. Just enjoy it. But we all know of cases where the rule just isn't true. It gets especially dicey when the stakes are high. Success rarely just sits there. Think of important relationships: husband-wife; player-coach; manager-employee. It's great to feel that things are going well, but the last thing you ever want to be is complacent. You have to keep trying to learn, to grow.

Or think of strategic goals. The plan that got you to one level isn't necessarily going to keep you there, or take you higher. The world is constantly changing, and so is your competition. One thing I've learned about the very best tennis players is that they're constantly thinking about their own game, and their competitors' games. They know that no matter how good they are, they have to adapt constantly to dozens of different factors—health (their own and their opponents'), weather, altitude, even different brands of tennis balls.

And they have to keep improving. Success at the highest levels of sport isn't just about maintenance. We've seen how a number of sports, tennis included, have improved over time: Well, what that really means is that the players keep getting better. And the easiest way to fall off that treadmill is to listen to your ego and assume all you have to do is just keep being you, wonderful you.

8. Change a Little, Change a Lot

Why the best can never stop trying to get better.

"Andy, I'd love to see you be in the top 10 in return games won. Can you take that challenge?"

—*B.G.*

I t goes without saying that Andy Roddick has one of the greatest tennis serves of all time. He has a terrific forehand. And—whether or not he happens to be number 1 in the world when you read this—there's a lot of room for improvement in his game.

I know Andy wouldn't argue with me on this. Not only is there a cluster of very tough, exciting players at the top of the rankings these days (whoever said that men's tennis was getting boring must be off somewhere eating his hat); Andy also happens to be, as of this writing, twenty-one years old. No one would argue that he's an amazing twenty-one-year-old, but God willing (and if Andre Agassi is any proof), Andy could have another dozen years or more of great tennis in him. He just has to improve; if he doesn't, others will.

This is another of the many lessons I learned from Andre. I told you that I felt from the first time I saw him (he was all of sixteen years old at that point, weighing in at around 120) that, as I like to put it, he hit the ball from

God. I've seen a lot of tennis, I have a good eye for the game, and I don't think anybody I've ever seen hits the ball better—cleaner, harder, earlier—than Andre Agassi.

But the first big surprise of our work together in 1994 (after I realized he didn't need to change a single part of his game) was that Andre wasn't satisfied with his game at all. Ten years later and, as of this writing, an astonishing number 5 in the world (at age thirty-three!), he *still* hits the ball from God. Yet in his mind, he's a long way from where he wants to be. He's the most driven-for-perfect player I've ever seen. He's a tinkerer by nature (with his forehand and serve. He never touches his beautiful, compact, two-handed backhand).

Where his serve is concerned, he's simply never satisfied. At five eleven and a muscular 180 pounds, Andre isn't exactly a shrimp, but most of the great servers (McEnroe being a notable exception) have been six feet or over. Andre just has never had the overpowering delivery of a Roddick (six foot three) or a Sampras (six one) or a Goran Ivanisevic (six five). And so he's always making adjustments to the serve, trying to add more power or kick, or get his legs into it more. At one point, he wondered whether, like Michael Chang (who is five foot nine), he should switch to a longer racquet. At Key Biscayne in 1996, he did try a longer stick for a couple of matches, but shelved it in the midst of the tournament. Amazingly, he went on to win the event.

Some days, after hitting a few on the practice court, he'd grin that big grin of his, and say, "I got it."

"What do you mean, 'I got it'?" I'd say.

"I got the new swing on my serve."

Now it was my turn to smile. "What do mean, you got the new swing on your serve? Did it come to you in the middle of the night?"

But his grin would get even bigger. "Yeah."

I would look at the new swing; and it would strongly resemble the old swing, with, perhaps, a slight adjustment to backswing speed. *Fine, Andre*, I would think. *Whatever works for you.*

Yet here's the weird thing: It did work for him. Nobody knew Andre's game like Andre. Suddenly he'd be sticking his serve, winning more points outright with it.

And so I came up with this crazy idea.

After our first half-year together, after he'd turned his game around miraculously and won his first U.S. Open, I wondered, *How can he get even better?* I had been Mr. Cruise Control in my career; I wanted to avoid any hint of it in Andre's. So I appealed to his perfectionism.

Everyone knows that Andre has the greatest service return of all time. One day he and I were looking at the ATP serve and return statistics, and—no surprise—Andre's name was all over the return stats. But he didn't have any numbers on the serve stats, other than first-serve percentage.

That's when I got my idea.

I thought that the one huge stat for Andre to be in on

was service games held. Predictably enough, the best in that category were all huge servers, from Sampras to Ivanisevic to Richard Krajicek. "Look," I said. "You don't have to blow people off the court to be a great server. Look at Johnny Mac—placement; spin; follow-up." My thinking was that if Andre could finish in the top three in that one category, he would have a very good year. You wouldn't have to look any further. His genius *return* of serve would ground the serving result.

I said, "Friendly wager—I bet you could get in on that stat, A.A."

Andre said, "I will be first."

And he finished 1995 in first place in holding serve. And he did have a monster year, winning a career-high seven tournaments, and advancing to number 1 for the first time—and staying there for thirty weeks.

There's nothing like a little challenge.

At the end of 2003, Andy Roddick was number 1 in the world, but meanwhile, Roger Federer was building on his Wimbledon win. Juan Carlos Ferrero was looking tough. Marat Safin, the Russian Bear, was emerging from hibernation. And Andre wasn't about to shuffle off to the retirement home.

It was tight at the top.

Now, Andy Roddick loves to play tennis. But when you're at the peak of the game, it's not always easy to keep that love clean and clear. There are a thousand different

pressures bearing down on you. Andy has worked unbelievably hard to get to the top, but he knows he's going to
have to work harder to stay there.

A big part of my job is keeping Andy focused on day-to-
day strategy. To figure out how to maintain his love for the
game and keep him improving at the same time. The box-
ers say, "If you're not trying, you're dying." They talk
about keeping your guard up. Well, my job is to be Andy's
guard. And the manager of his improvement.

A lot of this is time management. The more famous he
gets, the harder it is for him to move about the way he
used to when he was just Andy Roddick, the kid. There
are a lot more demands on his time—and that takes anybody time to get used to.

It's easy for all that to feel like a grind. Andy's trainer
handles the physical part of it, and great trainers are great
on-the-spot motivators. With the tennis, I have to be a little more strategic.

Yes, I'm good at on-the-spot—I love to get on the
court with Andy, stand at the net, and put him through
a few drills. The sound track is high-positive and high-
testosterone: "Yes! Crush it!" I yell. "More physical!" "Crosscourt!" "Down the line!" "Winner!" All the while, Andy
makes fun of me: my walk, my forehand (he says it's the
ugliest forehand he's ever seen).

But most of my work happens off the court. Vittles the
night before. At dinner, we're both relaxed, and I can

watch him carefully to figure out what information (and how much) he's in the mood for. But Andy's information isn't like Andre's. While both guys are outgoing and magnetic and fun to spend time with, they are very different tennis players.

Holding serve is clearly not the same kind of issue for Andy as it has been for Andre. It's barely an issue at all. (As is returning serve for Andre.) But at the end of 2003, I noticed that while Andy was number 1 in five of six serving categories, he was nowhere to be found in any one of the six categories for the return game.

And so, seeing that Andy was in a feisty mood while we were having dinner one night in November—it was during the Masters tournament in Houston—I said, "Andy, I'd love to see you be in the top 10 in return games won; can you take that challenge?"

He smiled, and I knew I had a taker.

There was nothing so tricky about my challenge. Andy and I both knew that if he could pick up his return game enough to get into the top 10, he would have a really good 2004. After all, if you're winning your serve almost all the time, and breaking the other guy's serve a lot of the time, you're winning most of the games, most of the sets, and most of your matches.

We also both knew that it was a heck of a lot more productive for me to say this than to mention anything about winning Slams or Super 9s—which I would never, ever do.

Talking about winning major tournaments is putting the cart before the horse, big-time. I know Andy wants to do it. I want him to do it. But hell, everybody else who's damn good wants it, too. A major is 128 guys, the luck of the draw, the weather, your health. I always say, every other day, you need to find a way to win three sets. And if all goes well, you can bang out twenty-one sets. That's the magic number for a major. It's also one of the hardest things to accomplish in sports. Improving Andy's return of serve was something we had control over, something we could go right out and start working on the next afternoon.

Which is just what we did.

Everybody can get better. The ego can't live on last year's results. In 1999, Andre Agassi was 29—bordering on old age for a professional tennis player. He'd been on the tour for more than thirteen years—as long as I had played it altogether. He had won Wimbledon once, the U.S. Open twice, the French Open once, and the Australian Open once. He could have legitimately started to slow down, or coast a little bit, or even hang it up. Nobody would have thought any less of him.

Instead, he decided to improve his movement on the court.

People—some smart people—told him, "You can't get faster at your age."

Andre said, "You know what? Getting faster isn't the whole story. The one thing I want is for people to talk about how I move *better* now than I ever have." And for a year and a half, he set about making his movement much more efficient. He knew that a lot of the great players, like McEnroe and Lendl, had lost a step when they got older, which opened up holes in their game. But the way Andre figured it, his game was never predicated on speed. Efficiency is a whole different story. Balance is a whole different story. And the reason he's still good is because of how efficiently he gets to the ball, how balanced he is when he sets up, and therefore how well he hits it. His movement hasn't become an issue. He hasn't lost a step—he's actually gained one. I think he moves better at thirty-three than he did at twenty-one! Amazing! (I think that improving movement—for everybody, pros and club players alike—is the huge new trend in the game.)

In his drive to make time his friend, Andre reminds me of John Elway and Barry Bonds. They're clearly not at the same physical peak as they were when they were twenty-one. But they are more intelligent now than they were then. They became better players as they got older because they figured out how to keep improving. Elway didn't have the same rifle arm at thirty-nine as he had at twenty-one, but he gained in accuracy. He stopped taking so many risks. He played smarter.

And Barry Bonds is unbelievable. When I was a kid,

great ballplayers like Willie Mays or Mickey Mantle were like broken-down prizefighters once they hit thirty-five. At thirty-nine—39!—Barry Bonds is putting eye to bat to ball better than ever. By working his butt off on his conditioning and his batting technique, he's become the most disciplined, feared hitter in baseball—the guy they seem to walk more often than not. I'm a big As fan, but I love Barry Bonds. However the media has portrayed him, I say he's must-see TV. I love his work ethic. I love his heart and dedication to getting better. I want to stand up and applaud a guy who, when they told him, "You can't get better at thirty-five," said, "Oh yeah?"

Not to mention the guy who when they told him, "You can't move better at twenty-nine," begged to differ. Andre taught me that everybody—even Andre—can get better. What I've slowly come to realize is that that also includes me as a coach.

> Doing a real service usually means working overtime.

I've always been a major talker. Maybe it has something to do with being the third child: When you come along at the end of the line, you want to make sure you don't get lost in the shuffle.

But I also like to think that the number of words that come out of my mouth have a direct relation to the number of ideas in my head. I may be wrong, I may be right, but I'm always thinking about things—all kinds of things—and I always have an opinion.

Naturally, a lot of what goes on in between my ears has to do with sports in general, and tennis in particular. I'm constantly amazed by how much there is to think about inside the 27 by 78 feet of the singles court, by how many new ideas there are in the game, no matter how long it's been around. The reason (of course) is the constant flow of new players. Which means new personalities, styles, matchups.

It's really exciting, and staying excited is what keeps me going. But one of the biggest lessons I've learned over the course of my coaching career is the wisdom of keeping some of my excitement inside.

It's not so easy for a naturally gregarious guy like me. Something Chiv showed me early on is why it's important not to get worked up over victories before the final round of a tournament. But a huge coaching lesson I've learned myself—and, frankly, one I've learned through my mistakes—is how to shut up and pay close attention to what my player is thinking, feeling, and saying. It's an ongoing project for me, and I hope I'm even better at it now than I was when I wrote these words.

9. Listen!

When you have a lot to say, shutting up is one of the hardest things in the world to do. And often one of the best. Try it.

"I think that's what Andre loved most about me. When he did ask my opinion, I gave it to him, short, straight, and honest."

—B.G.

My mom's dad was a Romanian immigrant who came to the States when he was two. Grew up and drove a taxi in San Francisco for forty years. Grandpa Morris was a simple guy. When I was a little kid, he used to drive me around in his cab; when I got to be a little older, he taught me how to drive. He knew my life was tennis, but he would never talk about tennis. He'd ask me about girls, discuss baseball or the weather. My grandpa was a great listener—I guess that's a skill you develop behind the wheel of a taxicab—and just an easy guy to be around. In many ways he was the opposite of my dad, who was always focused on my tennis and superintense about it, always the motivator.

Chiv was kind of like Grandpa Morris in some ways: quiet, easygoing, nonjudgmental. I always felt he was paying attention. He didn't ask me personal questions, but if I suddenly said I had a problem with a girl, for example, he'd listen and give me an opinion.

My dad formed me as a junior player. He helped make

me supertough, supercompetitive. I also had the benefit of playing a million matches with my older brother Barry and my older sister Dana, who was a top junior and a fine tour player. I had what Dad liked to call the fire in the belly. And those qualities propelled me through my pro career while other players—some of them just as athletically talented as me—fell by the wayside. When it came to my second career, my fire was still there, but I suddenly found I needed new qualities, too—the very ones Grandpa and Chiv had shown me. I learned to listen.

It may sound simple, but it isn't—especially for someone who likes to talk as much as I do. I told you earlier about the 1999 French Open, when I just about forced Andre to get therapy on his hurt shoulder and play the tournament when all he wanted to do was go home. Well, that could never have happened if we'd just started working together. In the spring of 1999, we'd been a team for five years, covered a lot of ground together, had a lot of ups and downs. I'd learned a lot over those five years—about Andre and about the job of coaching. And a lot of what I'd learned had to do with realizing when to keep my mouth shut and when to jump in.

Those lessons weren't always easy. There were times early on when I'd get excited about some idea I had had for Andre's match the next day, and Andre would get excited, too. Maybe Todd Martin was hitting his backhand crosscourt that week, and I'd come up with a counterplay for Andre. It's exactly the kind of technical discussion that Andre can get way into. If we were both watching a match on TV, we might find ourselves talking on the phone about it, my hotel room to his, five or six times in an evening. But there would be times, when I made that seventh call, when I'd suddenly find he had shut down for the night. "Okay, B.G., enough," he'd say. "No more tennis for the night." Sometimes I can overdo it.

Or sometimes, early on, we'd be at dinner, and I could see Andre was a little down about something, and I'd throw the hook out, see if we could get into a little strategic discussion. Occasionally he didn't pick up on it, but I continued on anyway, trying to work back to the subject. Well, there were times he'd say, "B.G., just stop; I don't want to talk about it."

At first, it hurt a little bit. But I got over that by realizing I needed to try not to take it too personally. I saw that Andre's being direct with me was respectful and, yes, helpful. It taught me more about who he was. And it clarified our relationship.

Another lesson I learned early on in my work with Andre was that no matter how much I knew about tennis, it was impossible for me to know everything. Andre needed guidance; he needed a lot of help strategizing his matches. But something in me realized right away that I couldn't just throw a game plan into his lap. Part of my job was listening to what he thought, too.

I might say something like, "Listen, if you work the backhand down the line to open the court tomorrow, you're going to be fine." But then Andre might answer, "How am I going to set that up? That's easier said than done."

My turn. "Well, I think if you use your forehand—whenever you have a chance, pound that forehand—then maybe the opportunity will be there."

And so instead of my telling him, "Go do this, do that," we'd analyze different scenarios together. We'd get to talking in depth about the opponent, the conditions, the whole climate of the match. It was a discussion, not a lecture. And naturally, the best time to do it was (and still is, with Andy) at dinner.

Now, that might sound like a business meal—an important meeting conducted over a few plates of unnoticed (and undigested) food. Very intense, furrowed brows, moving the peas and carrots around to describe the strategy on court.

That ain't me. I never wanted to be a drill sergeant. A huge part of coaching, for me, is being able to go out to dinner, have some beers, unwind, and have a fun time. Get away from the pressure itself. If we can't do that, then the bridge is stuck a little bit. Now, obviously we can't go out every night while we're on the road. There are going to be times (speaking of Andy now) when he'll want to have dinner with his girlfriend or some pals. But a big part of our working relationship is *never* getting into a pattern of saying, at the end of the work day, "I'll see you tomorrow."

Two guys, two cabs—no good.

I love fine food, and I love to go out for a great meal even—no, especially—when I'm on the job. When I'm traveling to a city, I can get excited days ahead of time just thinking about a favorite restaurant. (If Andy and I are going anywhere near Miami, I know immediately that unless somebody beats me off with a stick, I'm going to Joe's Stone Crab. Every other night.)

So it's all about relaxation. After we shoot the breeze a bit, I might say, "What do you think about maybe working the backhand down the line tomorrow?" I'll just toss a little hook out—I call it throwing a little bone. (Sometimes he'll throw it right back. And that's the greatest opportunity in coaching—I call it Go Time. When your player asks, "What do *you* think?" you really need to be ready to come on strong.) The next thing you know, we might find ourselves having a good twenty-minute conversation about what's going to happen tomorrow—if it truly is a relaxed dinner.

If things are tense, I'll know it in a minute. (When you're as close to your business partner as I am, you learn to read every flicker of his facial features, every shade of his voice.) Okay, then we take it down a little. Maybe we'll talk about other sports for a while—something fun, anything but business. This is my specialty: I'm the King of Spin. That's my job.

What it's really about is giving my guy space. And not judging myself if he really wants it. This is not the time to start thinking, "Jeez, he doesn't want to hang out with me." Chiv would always say to me about those situations: "Don't overthink it. Don't worry about it."

In other words, don't pick on it. Don't make it more of a problem than it is. Something could have happened with his girlfriend. Something could have happened with his parents. Pull back. Work with what you've got, and try to go from there.

At the same time, I try not to let his tension rule the evening. I'll stay upbeat, watch him carefully, try throwing that bone a couple more times. . . .

And then, sometimes, I see it's no use. Pushing the subject any further at this point is just going to be imposing my will. He's a little uptight about tennis now. I stay positive, but I change the subject. Maybe we need to wait till tomorrow—or maybe just later in the evening. Maybe the right moment will come up at 10:30, while we're in my room or his, watching *SportsCenter* or the basketball game. I've learned to pick my spots.

There was a lot of learning going on in the early days. The growing trust and communication between Andre and me in our first year led to his huge turnaround of 1994, which led in turn to his amazing 1995, a year he started off by beating Pete Sampras in the final of the Australian Open and then continued by putting together the most incredible summer any player had had in years.

During that summer, Andre won Washington, Montreal (beating Pete in the final), Cincinnati, and New Haven. Everyone said he was crazy to play four tournaments in a row. He won all four. He had won twenty-six matches in a row going into the final of the U.S. Open against Pete, who hadn't won a tournament all summer—except for Wimbledon.

As of that final, A.A. was clearly the number 1 player in the world. He would stay number one even if he lost the match. But this was one for the historians—whoever won it would have claimed two Grand Slams that year.

I thought Andre was clearly the better player coming into the final; I felt he should have won that match. He put his heart and soul into it. But Pete raised his level—he had a way of doing that every time he played; Andre thought that was his genius. Andre lost it 7–5 in the fourth, and something went out of him. He only played three matches the rest of the year, and lost his number-1 ranking because he didn't play. Pete passed him in the fall, and ended the year number 1 in the world.

I think a little part of Andre died after losing that final. He went out of 1995 still down and continued to slide for part of 1996. He was struggling on the court; I was beating myself up for not being able to help him more. A bad combination.

Andre is a complex guy. He's a genius athlete, and he's a warrior with a fierce competitive spirit. At the same time, I think it's fair to say that tennis is less of his life than it might be for other great champions. His family and his spiritual life come first. He also happens to have a truly brilliant mind (he has the most amazing recollection I've ever seen—he can summon up every point of an important match for years after he played it) and a huge curiosity about the whole world: not just sports but politics, music, art. Some people think he's aloof, but nothing could be less true. Fun is extremely important to him—something he has in common with Andy.

But Andre wasn't having any fun at the beginning of 1996, and neither was I. I kept telling myself we could weather the storm. Still, some part of me—a part I didn't show anybody—was worried.

I kept watching him, looking to find that spot—the moment where I could reach out to him, help him. I bit my tongue a lot. I just didn't want to get on Andre's case. I'd learned that when he was really edgy about something, it often didn't do any good to try to shake him out of it. Instead I would say, "Hey, if you need anything, if you want to rap about something, just call me."

And I'd leave it right there.

What I always tell the guy I'm working with is this: "The tennis court is 27 by 78 feet. I understand what goes on within those boundaries unbelievably well. If you want to talk about anything outside those lines, I'm glad to give you my opinion, but it'll just be my opinion."

Even if I thought (in the days before he was married), *Andre, you have to get rid of that damn girlfriend, you can't win a match as long as you're with her*—I would never say it. Ever. That would be stepping over the boundaries. I wouldn't want somebody to do that to me. It might work for a quick fix, but if you volunteer that kind of information, you will have a short coaching relationship because, sooner or later, I don't care how smart you are, you are going to say the wrong thing. It doesn't matter how close I am to the guy. There are some things you would never say to a close friend.

And when your friend is also your business partner, and he also happens to be signing your checks, things get complicated. You need to be yourself—that's what he hired you for. You don't want to waffle: He hired you to be decisive. But you don't want to say things you don't really believe, just to please him. The guys I work with are sharp enough to cut through that kind of stuff.

So you listen. And wait for your spot.

Only when A.A. would say, "What do you think?" would I then say, "Do you want me to tell you honestly? Okay, that's what I'll do." I think that's what he loved most about me. When he did ask my opinion, I gave it to him, short, straight, and honest.

But in early 1996, he wasn't asking my opinion about his tennis. I could see he was licking his wounds. And he was losing a lot of tennis matches to people he shouldn't lose to. It felt too close for comfort to the place he'd been just before he hired me.

Then he saw the Big Penny.

Let me explain. My house, north of San Francisco, was built a hundred years ago by the founder of Korbel Champagne. It's a great big turn-of-the-century mission-style house, and on the first floor, just past the foyer, there's a terrific old wooden bar, about twelve feet long, from late-eighteenth-century England. Man, I love that bar. I love to look at the old wood, run my fingers along it. It's a place where I like to just sit and think sometimes. And behind the bar, in a glass case, I have my bronze medal from the 1988 Olympics.

Whenever Andre would come over to my place, I noticed he would kind of stare at the medal. Then one day during that long period in early 1996, he asked me about it. "B.G., what's the deal with the medal, man?" he said. I'd mentioned to him somewhere along the line that I was still kicking myself for not winning the gold. So why was I showing off the bronze?

"Oh, man—the Big Penny," I said. "That's a saga."

Now it was Andre's turn to listen.

> If you keep your eyes on the prize, your feet are bound to find the holes in the street.

It's a cliché, but it's also very true that we learn much more from losing than from winning. Winning is about putting it together, using what we *have learned*. And often, winning is about being unconscious—in flow. Where the idea breaks down a little bit is in my favorite kind of victories: tough, gut-it-out, come-from-behind ones. Five-set victories where you lose the first two. Those really do teach you something.

But naturally—if you don't get derailed by excuses—defeat is the best teacher of all. The lessons you learn from losing are hard ones, though. It takes a lot of courage and concentration to look straight at a bad loss, figure out what it says about you, and put your conclusions to work. It keeps you from getting too full of yourself.

Wouldn't it be nice if our worst defeats just went away once we'd learned what we needed to learn from them? They do have a way of sticking around, though! I remember reading somewhere that medieval monks used to keep a skull on their desks to remind them of death. Well, I don't have any skulls around my house, but I've got the next best thing, in a glass case behind my bar.

10. The Big Penny

Sometimes failure is more precious than gold—or bronze, anyway.

"I had officially taken my eye off the ball."

—*B.G.*

This is the story I told Andre:

The biggest joy and the biggest disappointment in my whole tennis career came packed together in one event, the 1988 Olympics in Seoul.

Tennis was one of the events in the original Olympics, in 1896, but then after 1924, for a bunch of boring political reasons (everything is politics), it wasn't played as a medal sport again for sixty-four years. And so it made sense that when tennis was reinstated to the Games, a lot of attention got paid to who was going to be picked to play for the United States.

Late in 1987, when the Olympic Committee began to decide who would be on the American team, I was the second highest-ranked American player in the world. Jimmy Connors was a couple of spots above me, but Jimmy wasn't interested in playing. The Committee approached John McEnroe, but John didn't want to play, either. And a just-turned-seventeen-year-old by the name of Andre Agassi was beginning to blaze a path through the tennis world, but he was still (not for long) ranked far below Tim Mayotte and me.

And so Tim and I were chosen to play singles for the United States. It was an incredibly proud moment.

But soon after my semifinal loss to Lendl in the 1987 Masters, I came to a screeching halt.

I had always had problems with my feet and ankles, but this was the worst so far. Scar tissue had built up on a tendon in my left foot—the same tendon I'd injured way back when in Taipei—and now I had to have surgery. I was in a cast for weeks afterwards, and then I didn't play tennis for eight long months.

In the meantime, the sports press began to stir up a big fuss, saying the American team should consist of the old champ McEnroe and the young phenom Agassi (who was rising through the rankings every minute), instead of those two solid veterans Gilbert and Mayotte.

Even at seventeen, Andre was his usual gracious self. "Those guys have already got their spot," he said. "I'm fine." And John was also his usual self: He changed his mind and decided he'd like to play the Olympics.

Neither Tim nor I, however, wanted to give up our spot.

But it was tough. There I was hobbling around on crutches while McEnroe was fit, and the whole world seemed to be agitating for me to give way. I felt like I was fighting off demons, and I wasn't even at the Games yet.

I held on.

The Games were to take place in mid-September; I came back on to the tour in August. In my first five tournaments I didn't get past the second round. By the time I flew to Seoul, my confidence was in the crapper, and so were my spirits. I was feeling good and sorry for myself.

Then I walked in the official procession into the Olympic Stadium on the opening day of the Games.

I got goose bumps before I even knew what was happening. The American flag was flying in front of us; all around me, behind other flags, were the greatest athletes in the world. Wrestlers, shot-putters, pole-vaulters, sprinters, swimmers. This—I realized—was their big shot. They didn't get to go to Paris or Rome the next week; they didn't get to make any money, let alone the kind of money I was making.

I stopped feeling sorry for myself, fast.

I had what I now think of as my Andre Moment—the kind of moment he's had a number of times throughout his great career: He has always had a miraculous ability, unlike any player I've ever seen, to come back from anything on the strength of sheer willpower. I kicked my will into gear. I decided I was going to turn my year around right here, right now. I was going to get back to me. I was going to stop worrying about whether I was 65 percent.

I was still not moving anything like the way I could when I was at the top of my game. Every time I played, I had to wear an ankle brace and tape my foot heavily. I had to ice the foot down after every match. But I told myself that I was going to stop feeling sorry for myself about this foot, and just start playing.

I started playing well.

Then there was a lucky omen. Kim was seven and a half months pregnant when I went off to the Olympics: It was our first pregnancy, and we were very excited. She had to have some tests done, and during the middle of the tournament, I called her to see how they had gone. I called from a pay phone outside the Olympic Village—and on the phone next to me there was this little guy, a Kenyan distance runner, making the exact same call to *his* pregnant wife in Kenya! A true international moment. And at the exact moment Kim told me, "It's a boy!" (and I yelled, "Yes!"), the distance runner's wife said the same thing to him (and he yelled "Yes!"). The runner and I high-fived each other. My spirits had risen out of the dirt and into the sky.

The next thing I knew, I'd won four matches, beaten some good players. I was in the semis, up against my teammate, Tim Mayotte. Whoever won would play the victor of the other semi, between Miloslav Mecir, of the Czech Republic, and Stefan Edberg of Sweden.

After Mecir upset Edberg, I suddenly thought, *I'm going to win this thing. I'm going to get the gold.*

My confidence was way up again. I was on a roll, and I saw the glittering prize before me. Mayotte owned me so far in my pro career, but—matchups are weird—I had done much better than he had done on the tour. I had beaten him in college. I knew I could beat him now, and I thought my chances against Mecir were better than his.

That was probably my mistake. For one of the only times in my career, I got ahead of myself. In the vast majority of cases, I was—I still am—a nuts-and-bolts guy. An ice-in-my-veins strategic thinker, Mr. X's-and-O's. What I should have thought was this, and only this: *I need to win three sets in a best-of-five match against Tim Mayotte. How do I do it?*

Instead, I thought about the Gold. I remembered my goose bumps during that opening ceremony. Then I imagined myself standing on the highest platform at the closing ceremony, the medal being hung around my neck. I saw it all so clearly. . . .

The day of the match was a bummer. The event was held in the Stadium, a huge venue. I was a seasoned tour player, and usually I didn't think twice about playing a stadium match. Grubber that I was, usually I would just put on my hard hat and go to work: Gut out every point.

But this felt different. North Korea had sat out the event, and in Seoul, which was just thirty miles from the border, there was tension in the air. Security was high, attendance was low. When Tim and I played our match, the stadium was less than half full.

And then there was the fact that we were both Americans. The usual national spirit, our country against theirs, the very thing that makes the Olympics so exciting, just wasn't there. It was an early morning match. I let it all irritate me. And with the irritation, I got tight.

I didn't like that I was playing my teammate. And I have to admit it now, I didn't like playing Mayotte. He had beaten me in a bunch of close matches by always doing the same thing: coming in to net on me. Good serve, great volley. In to net. Again and again and again.

I thought, *Okay, I'm not going to let him do this. I'm going to get to net more. I'm going to take it away from him.* But my thoughts, so clear and sharp before the match, got muddled when I stepped out on the court. I was irritated, I was tight, I wanted the prize. I wanted to beat Mayotte without connecting the dots I needed to connect in order to win a match against him. I wanted the result more than any result I'd ever wanted before, and that made me edgy.

It was an unfamiliar feeling. My toughness ran deep, but suddenly I felt rattled. I thought, *Oh, well, he's uptight, too.* But as we began to play, I saw that he wasn't. In to net he came, and before I knew it we were playing his game, yet again.

Up to now, I'd always thought of myself as a big old American car, just tooling along the highway of professional tennis. I'd never worked extra hard for the big tournaments, not even the Slams. My attitude was always: If I lost, I just moved on. A tourney's a tourney. There was always another one next week.

All at once, here in Seoul, there was no next week. I

knew I might never get the chance to play in the Olympics again. And the brass ring—or I should say the gold—was hanging right in front of me. I knew, *knew*, I could beat Mayotte, and then Mecir.

I had officially taken my eye off the ball.

I'd always based my game on being methodical. There was nothing methodical going on in the match with Mayotte. It was all too reminiscent of that NCAA final against Mike Leach: Suddenly I found myself in an unfamiliar (not to mention uncomfortable and counterproductive) mode—playing not to lose.

I could always counterpunch with almost anybody. Almost nobody, with the exception of McEnroe and Lendl (and Brian Teacher, at the top of his game), ever blew me off the court. And Mayotte didn't blow me off that day. In the first set, I stayed right with him, until I was serving at 4–5. That was when I got what tennis pros call the Cement Arm. My mind was troubled, my muscles were tight, and my serve got weak. Mayotte put away the game and took the first set.

Unbelievably enough—or maybe I should say all too believably—the same exact situation came up in both of the next sets. My turn to serve at four games to five. Cement Arm. Mayotte breaks. Gilbert loses, 6–4, 6–4, 6–4.

Tim went on to get pretty well destroyed by Mecir in the final the next day. So he took home the silver, and Edberg and I both got the Bronze.

One Big Penny apiece.

Are you ready for the supreme irony? A month later, at the Paris Indoor, I beat both Mecir and Mayotte, in the round of 16 and the semifinals, respectively.

It helped. But it still didn't take away the sting of the worst defeat of my career.

Andre stared at the Big Penny. I tried to explain my mixed feelings about the Games. That one match was a disaster for me; yet at the same time, those two weeks in Seoul were, in many ways, the pinnacle of my career. They'd never had tennis in the Olympics when I was a kid, and here I was, playing in them!

The whole thing made me feel as gee-whiz as a kid: To be around all those amazing athletes, and to watch them in action (I went to every event I could possibly attend); to walk into the Stadium with Carl Lewis and all the great players on our basketball team; to stay in the Olympic Village, rather than just in some hotel.

I never heard my name mentioned for the whole two weeks. It was always, "Game, U.S.A.," or "Game, Spain." "United States, bronze medal." You never heard your name! It felt like being in your own private History Channel. It was all incredibly moving.

And then I tried to tell Andre my feelings about the Penny itself. I said that if I could push a button and make one change in my tennis career, I would have won the Gold. I told him that I walk by my bar every day, and there are times when I can look at that medal and times that I can't. Sometimes, even after more than fifteen years, the pain is just too sharp. Other times, though, I look hard at that Penny and feel so proud to have been a part of the Olympics, to have been able to play for my country. What does my little defeat matter, compared to all that? I think, *What is, is. Live with it. Learn from it.*

It's been said a million times, but it's so true: It's very rare that we learn from victory.

As Andre's 1996 season went from bad to worse, he spent a lot of time over at my house, and I kept catching him staring at the Big Penny. Then one day, he said, "You know what, B.G.? If I don't win anything else this year, I'm going to win the Gold at the Olympics."

And you know what? It wasn't easy—in fact, it was just about as hard as everything else was for him that year—but that's exactly what he did. He just stepped up and played great. I'm not ashamed to tell you that I had to wipe away a couple of tears when Andre finally held that medal up.

I was so proud of A.A. for stepping up. It was an amazing two weeks: It made his whole year, and it would be a memory for his whole life. I told him, "Man, I can't believe you could sleep with that medal every night if you wanted."

Andre told me he'd let me sleep with his medal whenever I felt like it.

> What is, is. Live with it. Learn from it.

Competing head-to-head is always going to stir up strong emotions, especially when there's money and testosterone involved, and every major competitor has to figure out how to deal with anger. In our sport, there have been a handful of people who could use fury to fuel their best performances, but they're the exceptions, by far. The vast majority of us—I include myself—get thrown off our game when we lose our tempers.

Anger in a competitive situation is about fear of losing control. And inconveniently, it builds on itself: The madder we get, the more out-of-control we get. It comes when we're not in flow, which means we're trying too hard. It would seem to follow, then, that in order to play well, we should try less. Unfortunately, things aren't always that simple.

I've found that the best way to attack the problem of anger, in myself and my players, is to get at the root causes beforehand. The best way to avoid feeling out of control is to have a game plan—and a backup, and a backup

backup. Method and flexibility lead to coolness under fire.

And naturally, the best way to come up with a game plan is to put your head together with a trusted coach who knows your game as well as you know it yourself. When ego flares up into anger, it's a safe bet that a player isn't just feeling out of control: He (or she) is feeling alone out there. A true team player is much less likely to be afraid.

11. Method Before Madness, or Trial by Error

Somewhere around a corner on your path to greatness, someone or something is lurking that will make you nuts.
Slow down, and get to greatness faster.

"Do you need an arm to hit?"

—*B.G. to Andy Roddick*

ome tennis players are driven by anger. There's a
primitive logic to it: Besides boxing and wrestling, singles tennis is the only form of single combat in sports,
and when it's two guys slugging it out out there, you can
almost smell the testosterone. Wouldn't it make sense,
then, that each player should hate the other, and that—
given a certain level of skill—the player with more fury
should win?

Well . . . no. Tennis isn't boxing. You're 78 feet away
from the other guy (although that distance can close fast
if both of you come in to net); there's a racquet and a ball
involved, and a ton of technique. Sheer firepower can win
a match, but very often a smart player can defeat it with
speed, spin, tenacity, and strategy. I'm living proof of that.
(So are my four victories out of the first five times I played
Boris Becker.)

But when you're out on the pro tour, playing a game
that is, even at the highest levels, essentially frustrating,
against a bunch of guys who are basically trying to take

away your kids' lunch money, tensions can build up. And some players just can't chill out. For better or worse (and almost always worse), anger is just part of their playing vocabulary.

This has been true since the game's earliest days—although way back when, competitive tennis had a country-club veneer of good manners. But there were veneer-busters long before McEnroe or Connors. From the 1940s through the 1960s, the great Pancho Gonzalez, who had scraped his way up from wrong-side-of-the-tracks Los Angeles, was the angriest man in the game. Toward the end of Pancho's day, there was also a guy you've probably never heard of, a doubles specialist named Bob Hewitt.

Hewitt was an Australian who migrated to South Africa (some say because he fell in love with a South African girl; some say because the Australian tennis establishment had had enough of him), with a ferocious reputation on the court and off, which I got to witness in person, at age ten, when I ball-boyed for a pro tournament at Golden Gate Fields, a racetrack in San Francisco.

I got paid five dollars a match, big money when you're ten, and as a bonus, I was allowed to be the let judge on some matches. This meant that I would stand next to the umpire's chair with my hand on the top of the net, so that if a serve so much as ticked the tape, I would feel the vibration, and call out, "Let!"

It was a quarterfinal singles match, and the great In-

dian player Vijay Amritraj, then only seventeen and playing one of his first pro tournaments, was up against Hewitt. I remember the weather was terrible, very windy, and
Vijay and Hewitt had battled down to a tense tiebreaker in
the third and deciding set. It was 4–all in the breaker—
that was match point by old-fashioned nine-point tiebreaker rules—and Hewitt to serve. I was standing with
my hand on the net tape, not looking at anything but that
net, all my concentration on it. I heard the thwack of
Hewitt's serve, I heard him grunt, and then I felt the net
vibrate ever so slightly. My hand moved.

"Let!" I called out, in my high, ten-year-old voice.

Well, little did I know that Hewitt had served an outright ace to Vijay—but, because the wind had made it impossible to hear the ball brush the top of the net, I was the
only person in that stadium who knew the serve had been
a let.

Hewitt—a scary-looking guy to begin with, big and tall
and bald, with a black beard—went berserk. He stomped
in toward the umpire's chair, waving his racquet menac-
ingly and yelling. Then he got right in the face of the
umpire, a kindly, gray-haired gentleman named Warren
Wertheimer. Hewitt grabbed Mr. Wertheimer by the arm—
the match should have been over then and there—and
kept screaming at him. "That was a bloody, goddamn ace!"
he yelled, along with other words a ten-year-old shouldn't
have heard.

In the midst of it all, the umpire leaned down to me and said, "Are you sure it was a let?" I said, "I'm sure as day—that was a let." And Mr. Wertheimer said, "Yeah, I thought it was a let, too." Well, now Hewitt really went nuts—he hauled off and threw his wooden Dunlop Maxply straight at the umpire. (Fortunately for Mr. Wertheimer, his chair had a footrest in front of it, which partially deflected the racquet.) Default for Hewitt; game, set and match for Vijay, who went to the semifinals. And Hewitt proceeded to go even more nuts. It was quite a sight. When I finally left the court, he actually came after me—a ten-year-old kid!—and my dad had to come out of the stands to defend me. The two of them almost went at it then and there. I believe Hewitt was ultimately fined $5,000—a lot of money in 1971—and suspended from the tour.

But wait—that's not the end of the story. In 1983, I was playing my first Wimbledon. I had won the first round, and I was in the locker room getting treatment on my ankle, and Bob Hewitt, who was playing the Seniors event there, was also in there, also getting treatment. He was older, heavier, balder, but he was still just as surly, snarling at everyone in sight.

I was a long way from ten years old now, at my full size of six one and 175 pounds, and I wasn't especially scared of this old, heavyset guy. So with a smile, I introduced myself, shook his hand, and told him the story of that 1971 match at Golden Gate Fields.

And would you believe it, the guy got mad all over again about that let call! He glared at me in the Wimbledon locker room like he was ready to go after me again—except that I looked at him right back, and he quickly reassessed the situation.

All of which goes to show you that while anger might make for a good story or two, it almost never wins tennis matches, or much of anything else. Anger is a sideshow to the main event, and usually a distracting one. Connors and McEnroe were the only two people in my lifetime who could play better tennis after losing their tempers, and both competed in an era when the rules for on-court behavior were more lenient (and especially more lenient for Jimmy and John, who could intimidate tournament officials just by threatening not to come back to the event). And both were somehow able to refocus even more sharply after throwing a tantrum—a tantrum that almost always threw their opponent off his game. (I was that opponent on several occasions.)

But Mac and Connors were the exceptions. Everybody else—certainly me when I played, and definitely Andy, when he was just coming up—gets derailed by losing it. It's one thing to smash a racquet or two in the locker room, or back at the hotel. It's another thing to do it on the court.

When we started working together, Andy's temper was one of the big issues. His first coach is a good guy who accomplished a lot of things with Andy from the juniors through his first couple of years on the tour, but we have a different approach to coaching. He would tell Andy, "Go sit in your room and think and think and think, and then come out of the room and become a lion." He would try to work him into a rage. The only problem is, that's not an effective part of Andy's personality. He's a supercompetitive, superintense guy: He goes a hundred miles an hour 24/7, and he wants to win at everything he plays, from Ping-Pong to pool to Xbox. (And unfortunately, he can beat me at all of them.) He doesn't need anger on top of that. His old coach's strategy would get Andy stoked up; but often, if anything went off the rails during an important match, he would crash and burn.

I sized up Andy's nature before we ever worked together, and I saw it was very similar to Andre's. They're both great people. When you're around A.A., you will have fun. The same is true of Andy. (Although I didn't know, early on, that a lot of the fun was going to consist of Andy making fun of me.) One of the first things I said to Andy when our professional relationship began was, "Dude, let's go out every night for a good dinner." He said, "Yeah!" I could see the relief all over his face. No more lions.

Andre's attitude has always been, "Why do I have to be mean to people to be mean on the court?" He separates the two. When he is on the court, he's always been able to channel his aggression so purely into the tennis itself that none of it spills out onto himself or the other player. I helped him to learn that if he prepares properly and concentrates totally on the job at hand, his talent will take care of the rest. Method before madness.

I felt Andy needed more of that.

Early on, I told him, "Listen—if you get really mad, just hit me in the shoulder—the left shoulder." Careful, coach! Sometime later, Andy had around eight people pulling at him about different business matters (the more you succeed, the more of that stuff there is), and I could see he was upset. I said, "Do you need an arm to hit?" Well, Andy is a big, strong guy, and he really let me have it—but afterwards there was a huge smile on his face. "I'm okay now," he said.

"That makes one of us," I told him, rubbing my shoulder.

He knew I was kidding. (Mostly.) But he also knew I was serious on the first day we ever worked together, when I said, "No matter what, I've got your back. Whatever it is. And when you're going into battle, I'm there."

One day when he bounced his racquet in anger during a practice, I took the opportunity to say, "Look. Let's try fifty-five today. Safe and solid—like driving fifty-five miles an hour. Just look at me whenever you're about to get mad, and I'll do this"—I put my fingers to my temples, meaning, K.I.T. Keep it together, and your game will take you out of the tense situation. If your brain takes you out of the game, it's hard for your game to bring you back to where you need to be. Even if you're a great player, miracle shots will only get you so far.

"How often do you win when you get that angry?" I asked Andy.

He smiled. "Not too often," he said.

So we had a start. Andy understood K.I.T., and he knew that when he got to this neurotic place, his win level dropped dramatically. I told him I had been the same way. I acted like an idiot many times during my playing career. But—I call it Trial by Error—I learned from my own mistakes, learned from watching McEnroe (there were times when his anger took him to another level, but there were also occasions when his fury was just a symptom of what was going wrong—and kept getting more and more wrong—in a match).

I told Andy that Andre was pretty calm on the court, which helped his game get to another level, but even he would explode sometimes. We dealt with it—calmly. Always, my benchmark was Chiv: Whatever happened, no matter how bad, I knew that the one thing Chiv wouldn't do was start yelling at me. He knew it wouldn't help. He knew we needed to talk about the game. Maybe, somewhere in whatever had led to my explosion, there was a missed opportunity. Chiv would immediately forget about the incident itself. Instead, he'd say something like, "You know what? I think the reason you got in trouble is that you didn't work his backhand enough. The next time you play him, I think you need to use your forehand and dominate the court more. Take some more risks."

Sometimes, though, risk-taking alone doesn't cut it. Everybody loses—I don't care who you are, Andy Roddick or Tiger Woods or Alex Rodriguez or Michael Jordan. There are days when your overpowering talent is underpowered. Your serves are just missing the lines. Your approach shots are finding the bunkers. Your cutoff play is off. You're throwing bricks from the three-point zone.

But the really great champions usually find a way to compensate. If Jordan went 3 for 19 in a given game, the thing that separated him from anybody else is that he would still put his glove on and shut down the other guy's number 2 scoring guard. Because he stank that day didn't mean that he was going to complain to everybody; it meant he was going to play defense, get some rebounds and assists. If Alex Rodriguez goes 0 for 4, he's likely to make nine sparkling infield plays—as opposed to the lesser player who goes 0 for 4 and makes two errors just because he's sulking. And if that other A-Rod, Andy Roddick, is having an off day with his serve, he'll find a way to serve competitively anyhow, to put some more spin and placement into the equation, and to sharpen his return so there's more pressure on the other guy.

But what about the rest of us nongeniuses? Not to mention the geniuses on the days they can't even manage to put together Plan B? Every professional tennis player, even at the highest levels of the sport, has lost a match 6–4, 6–7, 0–6—the kind of match where you win the first set; then, after you blow a couple (or more) match points in the second, the other guy scratches and claws his way to taking the set (and maybe it was ugly; maybe the guy won it on a bad call), and then something in you just snaps. You go on walkabout—you basically tank the third set, because you just can't stand to be there anymore.

Happens to everyone sometimes. And it's bad.

What do *I* do, though, when I have to coach that player?

I don't scream. I've seen coaches really ream a guy out for losing a match that way—maybe because they're worried about how bad it made *them* look. (If I were them, I'd worry about how bad it made me look to be screaming that way.)

It's at moments like these that my inner Chiv kicks in. The first questions I ask my guy about a match like that are: What happened in the second set that led you to snap in the third? And what can we do to keep it from happening again?

Then I make sure I have some sort of plan to talk about it civilly later. Sometimes, after a match that bad, I won't even walk into the locker room for a while. When I do go in, my guy is usually very, very quiet. (Any racquets that needed to be smashed have already been smashed.) Then

I'll ask him if he needs something—a drink; anything at all. And then it's just, "Talk to you later." When he's calmed down; when I've calmed down. (Sometimes losses like that make me mad, too. But those are feelings I have to put aside: That's not what the partnership is about.)

When we're at dinner and the time seems right, we'll discuss the match. (Call it Vittles the Night After.) Blame is out of the equation. The talk is serious but positive. But it's also very direct. It's along the lines of, "Let's figure out what happened with those match points at 5–4 in the second. What were you doing well up until then, and what did you stop doing? I've been there myself plenty of times. What it looked like to me was that you hoped he was going to lose. You hoped he was going to give it to you. You didn't try to be aggressive. You let him be aggressive. You got too tentative. The next time that happens, let's take a little more risk, and if you're nervous on your forehand, let's take it out of the equation a little bit—let's serve-and-volley." (Once again, note the pronoun. It's *we* for coaching, *he* for playing. I told you about the coaches who say, "we won" and "he lost." Well, in my book, *he* wins or loses a match because *he's* the one playing it. The *we* part is getting ready. Team time.)

If I'm doing my job right, here's what I hope is going through his mind at that moment: *He's not harping on how I snapped.*

I know he snapped. He knows he snapped. Everybody

snaps sometimes. Talking too much about it just distracts us from the main point, which is: It *does* happen sometimes. So let's be methodical about reducing those occurrences.

A lot of players look away almost superstitiously from a bad loss. They're afraid to admit it happened, scared to admit that they have that chaos inside. They'd much rather say, "He played good, I played bad, the hell with it, forget about it."

After Andy lost to Tim Henman in the semifinals of the Paris Indoor in the fall of 2003, he was mad—and I mean *really* mad. It wasn't that he snapped, it was that he failed to raise his game at a moment when it really counted. (And I think I had failed to help him in a couple of ways, too: More about that in the next chapter.) If he'd gotten through Henman in that match and won the tournament, he would have put a little more space between himself and everyone else in the world.

But he didn't. Bad outcome. Andy smashed a couple of racquets after that match, and went out on the town in Paris to forget about the whole thing. And even after I'd waited what felt like a decent amount of time to bring up what went wrong in that incredibly close match—Henman played as well as he possibly could and won it in two tight tiebreakers—Andy said to me, "This didn't happen. I don't want to talk about it; this match didn't happen. I wasn't here tonight."

It took him a week to settle down and admit that it *did*

happen, and talk about it. He's different from Andre that way, but we work with it. (And why should every genius be alike?)

Andy knows that it really did happen. And he knows that I'll only give him about a week of pretending it didn't. And we both know that players who sweep their bad losses under the rug are the players who don't think, who don't strategize, who have little chance of moving to the next level—whatever that level may be.

One thing that has helped me move to the next level as a coach has been learning to coach women. Doing some work a few years ago with Mary Pierce and Martina Hingis (this was during my time with Andre, and he was totally cool about it) gave me a sharper appreciation for the purely strategic and psychological aspects of the game, and brought me out of the Neanderthal cave I used to occupy when I was a player. (Out of competitiveness and knee-jerk sexism, a lot of male players whine about how boring women's tennis is. Where the upper levels of the game are concerned, they're dead wrong—a lesson I'm happy to have learned, both as a husband and the father of two daughters.)

Working with female players helped me to relax my high standards a little. I couldn't tell Martina Hingis I wanted her to play like Andre Agassi. But I also couldn't cut corners: When it came to getting coffee or tennis balls or doing any of the little things I'd ever do for Andre, I knew I needed to do it, and enjoy it, for whomever I was coaching. One more step toward Chiv-hood: More patient. Less judgmental.

Anyway, whatever you may think about the differences between men and women, I'm here to tell you that anger is also a factor in women's tennis.

From time to time I work with Tatiana Golovin, a sixteen-year-old Russian girl now a citizen of France. Tatiana is one gutsy girl—I was amazed that she, and not her agent, was the one who called and asked me to work with her in the first place—and she's taught me even more about women's tennis. I'm teaching her a little bit, too.

I think Tatiana has huge potential, but when I watched her at Wimbledon last year, I didn't like the way she was playing. We had worked on a number of things the previous fall, and I felt she had regressed. Once again, she was hitting off her back foot, getting too far behind the baseline against some opponents she should have come in to net on.

I also thought Tatiana was being too dour. She was throwing her racquet a little too often, putting her hand on her hip, showing frustration. There's a difference between temperament (spirit) and temper. Every player flares up from time to time, but if you start to do it too much on court, it lifts your opponent's spirits, makes them feel they're getting under your skin.

I didn't get to see much of Tatiana at the 2003 U.S. Open—understandably, my attention was on Andy—but what I did see told me she was doing the same things. And so literally the day after Andy won the tournament, I had her fly back to California with Kim and me. We walked out onto my court bright and early the morning after we arrived. "Tatiana," I said, clapping my hands, "let's go to work."

I told her that she had lost her match at the Open because as soon as she got behind 3–1 in the first set, she got mad instead of concentrating. Instead of focusing on *Maybe I should attack her forehand—what should I be doing out here to construct a match?* she lost to herself. I told her: "Anger is a slippery slope, and it's almost always downhill. Everybody gets mad sometimes. If you do, try to get through it fast. Otherwise, you're going to blank out. Happens to everyone sometimes, and it's no good. Your feet start moving slow, and the match starts moving very quickly—zip, zip, you lose point by point.

"Get through the anger fast," I said, "but slow down the match—I call it taking a long, slow walk with yourself. Tell yourself you need a happy place. When I was younger, I'd hum a tune in my head—Tom Petty was good to me."

I pointed to my head. "Or play a few mind games with yourself," I said. "If you blow a game, but you're still up 5–4, tell yourself you're down 4–5, and you have to battle back. Or, if you win the first set and blow the second, take your forefinger, draw a box on your forehead and pretend you're erasing everything in there. Forget about it—and remember what got you ahead in the first place. Anger will make you stop thinking. Clear it out and start thinking again."

"You're not going to play a perfect point every time," I told Tatiana. "That's why we come out here and work on shots, work on technique—to get things better. But when you miss two or three backhands, don't hit the panic button, don't get mad, don't say, 'She's so lucky.' It's like giving the other girl hope that she's going to beat you today.

"And if she does beat you, and it's a bad loss, see what you can get out of it. It'll take time—maybe a day, maybe a month—before you can think about the match clearly, but when you can think about it, figure out all the things you're going to do different next time. Allen Fox used to say, 'Try to turn something bad into something good.' "

A footnote about my work with Mary Pierce: I think if I had it to do over again, I would do it differently. The reason I get along so well with Andre and Andy is that like me, they are gregarious guys—talkers, good at processing a lot of words. Mary is a quieter person, and I wish I'd done a better job of reading her in the first place. I may have overwhelmed her with verbal input. I think she tried to adapt to me, but really, I should've tried to adapt to her. I should've listened better.

On the other hand, I think realizing all this has made me a better coach to Tatiana.

> Anger is a powerful force in competition, but—think about it—is impossible to separate from fear.

If there's one thing I hope I've gotten across to you in this book, it's how important it is to love what you do. I've always played for high stakes—in my college career, my days on the pro tour, and my coaching—but I didn't begin to really excel until Chiv showed me the way. He wasn't what you'd think of as a classic motivator: He didn't have an ounce of rah-rah in him. He wanted to win as much as the next guy, but unlike so many guys, winning had nothing to do with ego for him. With Chiv, it was all about quiet and calmness, generosity and love for the game.

I'm not a naturally quiet guy. I'm a fiery, intense competitor. Maybe a different kind of coach could have charged me up more, but I think it would have ultimately been superficial. It wouldn't have taken me as far. I needed to learn to go deep down inside myself to get through the many challenges I would face as both a player and a coach.

I could be cocky when I was a junior player, but by the time I first met Chiv, I'd been taken down a notch. I'd hit the wall. Some drill-sergeant-type coaches try to take a player apart and then put him back together—they try to force humility. The relationship is a power struggle.

Chiv took the power struggle off the table. He showed me, by his example, that when you're pursuing an important goal, true humility isn't weakness but strength. He made a man of me, not by toughening me up but by giving me the best possible example of what a man could be.

I know I haven't always lived up to that example. But there's one lesson Tom Chivington taught me that, I'm proud to say, I've never failed at—not once, not for a single second: He showed me how to really love this great game.

I hope he understands how grateful I am for that.

12. You *Really* Gotta Love It

Love breeds humility: There's always more to learn. The work is never over at five o'clock.

"Yeah, I'm happy. I don't want to be number 1."

—*A top player who shall go nameless*

Tom Chivington taught me to love tennis, and also how to love myself a little more, too. I was a work in progress when I arrived at Foothill, with a long way to go, both as a player and as a human being. Another coach might easily have seen me as too much of a project. My years of grinding it out on the junior tennis circuit had made me tough and clever, but they hadn't made me especially wise. I lacked discipline, and deep down, I lacked a true feeling for what I was doing. I never hated it; I just think I didn't love it enough. The truth is, I was a little bit machinelike at age eighteen. And my inner clock needed to be reset. I was on Brad Time. If you told me to show up at two o'clock, and if I got there at 2:20, I thought I was doing all right. I needed to be recalibrated.

Chiv's genius was in knowing exactly how to change me. There was only one thing he could order me to do, and that was to be on time. And he said it so calmly, so matter-of-factly, that I knew I could never be late again.

But as for the rest, he did it with love. I don't know what

made him pick me out as a kid who would be receptive to his style of coaching: In a lot of ways, we were as different as two people could be. Physically; emotionally. Where Chiv was calm, I was hot-blooded. Where he said a little, I often said too much.

He saw my quirks. Yet from the beginning, he extended a hand of warmth. He and Georgie opened up their home to me. Chiv told me that if I needed anything, just to let him know, and he would try to take care of it for me. And it wasn't just good manners: It was all real. I felt genuine love coming from this man.

And something remarkable began to happen to me. I don't think it was any accident that I grew almost half a foot in my first six months at Foothill: My physical growth matched what was going on inside. My inner chaos was beginning to straighten out. When Chiv ordered me (softly) to be on time, I got punctual overnight—and discovered that since being on time made others like me better, it made me like myself better. When he took extra time on weekends to work with me on my backhand, I had to improve to make his sacrifice worthwhile.

I _had_ to grow to justify his faith in me.

Chiv taught me to rise to the occasion. To raise my game in every sense of the word. To (try to) become more like Chiv.

My new punctuality happened right away, my new backhand and my growth spurt took a few months. But the rest took years. It was only when Chiv began to travel with me part-time on the tour that I started to understand the true depth of his love and commitment. It's the kind of thing that just can't be faked. The kind of thing that all the rah-rah, drill-sergeant, X's-and-O's coaches in the world can never come close to, because there's no formula to it. You couldn't put it on a video: Quick Tips to Be Like Chiv! Wouldn't happen. There was a real humility to the man that came from his genuine love for his work. Love breeds humility: There's always more to learn. The work is never over at five o'clock.

I felt his humility and his love when he never—and I mean never—showed the slightest negativity after I blew a pro match. I'm not just talking about anger or annoyance, I'm also talking about disappointment. *Chiv was never disappointed.* Maybe part of it was that—unlike so many coaches, who are never-wases and wannabes living through their pupils—Chiv had an honest sense of his own limitations as a player. But along with that went an amazing eye for the game—sharp enough to see that I potentially had a pretty good eye myself. He always knew exactly where I had gone wrong in a blown match. His calm analysis, never blaming, usually kept me from making the same mistakes twice.

It also kept me from making excuses. The pro tour, especially at the lower levels, is full of excuses. As I moved up in the ranks, I was constantly aware of guys whining that they'd lost matches because of their shoes, their strings, the officiating, whatever. But Chiv was so clear about all the factors that caused a match to go south that I had to meet his standard. I had to be totally honest. I hope you feel I've been that honest with you in this book.

And part of being honest meant never, ever blaming Chiv for my losses. That "We won, he lost" thing some coaches say cuts two ways: A player can also say about his coach, "I won, we lost." Maybe the coach just wasn't coaching well enough; maybe he missed something. It couldn't have been *all* my fault.

If I'd ever been tempted to go that way (and I wasn't), I wouldn't have had a leg to stand on. Chiv was so hardworking and perceptive in his scouting of my opponents that I always felt prepared for my matches. If I didn't step up, I didn't step up. End of story.

I've tried to emulate him in my coaching career, but there've been a few speed bumps along the way. (I wince when I think about some of them, but ... Honesty! Humility!)

Early on with Andre, I can recall several occasions when I bantered too much—tried to cheer him up when he didn't want to be cheered up, or kept trying to work the strategy out when I could tell that he wasn't there. Those were tough days. *Chiv would never have done that*, I thought afterwards—until it began to dawn on me that I shouldn't (and couldn't) try to *be* Chiv, that I had to try to be the best possible version of myself, a guy who had learned *from* Chiv.

And there were scouting errors, too. At least a couple of times, I remember telling Andre about a certain player, "The guy cannot serve wide under pressure"—and then, of course, it turned out that that one day of the match, he was cranking out can openers left and right.

Then, in my first summer with Andy, there was Cyril Saulnier.

Saulnier was a Frenchman, ranked something like 120 in the world. I'd barely heard of him and never seen him play, but early in 2003, before Andy and I had started working together, Saulnier had given Andy a brutal match in Key Biscayne, which Andy had finally gutted out, 6–7, 7–6, 6–4. Then at the RCA Championships in Indianapolis, in late July, Andy was going to go up against Saulnier in the second round, so I'd gone and scouted the guy's first-round match. I'd immediately noticed his backhand—Saulnier was ripping every single one crosscourt, and just killing his opponent with them. So that's what I told Andy that night at dinner: "Watch out for this guy's crosscourt backhand."

Okay, now you know what's coming, right? The next day, this French guy ripped fifteen stone-cold backhand winners—down the line. After Andy had lost the first set and was down a service break in the second, he looked up at me in the stands and yelled out, "Crosscourt backhand, huh?" I slumped lower in my seat than I've ever slumped before. (Fortunately, Andy went on to come back in the second set and win the match—and the tournament.)

Maybe inconsistency is why Saulnier was 120 in the world. Or maybe not. Another lesson I learned from Chiv (and Andre and Andy) is that the top guys aren't at the top just because of their tennis skills—they're thinking, too. They change; they adapt. Even against a player like Todd Martin, whom he beat far more often than not, Andre always wanted to know what the guy was doing *that week*. Was he placing his serve differently? Hitting more down-the-line forehands than usual? It was always worth the time for me to go out and watch. I might not see anything. But if I saw one little thing, it could alter the outcome of a match.

And most important for me, there's nothing I love doing more than sitting and watching a tennis match, analyzing exactly what's going on out there. (They say that love is blind, but my love for tennis makes me extremely observant.) Some guys like fishing, some like woodworking, some like to take apart car engines. I like to take apart tennis matches. I think I always have.

In the quarterfinals of last year's U.S. Open, Andy was going to play the winner of the match between Sjeng Schalken of the Netherlands and Germany's Rainer Schuettler. The match was on one of the outside courts at Flushing Meadows, and weirdly enough—maybe it had something to do with all the rain delays they had during that tournament—there were about nine people in the stands. One of whom, very conspicuously, was yours truly, Mr. Scout.

During the warm-up, Schalken looked over at me and said, "I can't believe you're watching me—you've seen me play so many times!"

Well, there were two things he had failed to take into consideration. First, that I'll scout anybody who has a chance of playing my guy, no matter how often I've seen him play, because something might be different this time. And second, there were two players on that court. What made Sjeng so sure I was there to watch *him*? In fact, Andy had lost both matches he'd played with Schuettler that year, and since both had happened before my tenure, I hadn't seen them. I didn't know Schuettler's game nearly as well as I knew Schalken's.

What I loved was that *neither* guy was exactly sure who I was out there to look at. There I was in my shades and Metallica hat, and nobody knew. I knew, though. I was scouting both of them. And having the time of my life.

My job is a strange one, beginning with the question of whether it's even necessary. As you might expect, the majority of professional tennis players travel without a coach—in many (if not most) cases, because it just costs too much money. Make no mistake, the top hundred touring pros earn plenty, but they also spend plenty. It costs heavily to travel thirty-plus weeks of the year, and while players at the very top of the men's and women's games often bring along small entourages—girlfriend or boyfriend, trainer, nutritionist, coach—the economics of traveling with company are daunting for anyone below the peak of the mountain, which is to say, anyone who isn't earning millions in endorsement money.

Beyond the question of money, though, who needs a traveling coach? Several great champions of the recent past never had one: Ivan Lendl, John McEnroe, Jimmy Connors. And most of the great players of the pre-Open era—people like Bill Tilden and Don Budge and Pancho Gonzalez and Jack Kramer—were strictly solo players in a single-combat sport. Some of those tough old guys (I've known a few of them) would've hooted you off the court if you'd mentioned the idea of a coach.

On the other hand, the Australians dominated the tennis world in the fifties and early sixties mostly through the guidance of one of the game's great coaches, Harry Hopman. (Hopman even had a hand in the early development of John McEnroe.) And then there were key figures like Lennart Bergelin, who traveled with Bjorn Borg, making Borg's amazing dominance of the late seventies possible; and Ion Tiriac, who coached Ilie Nastase, Guillermo Vilas, and for a brief time, Boris Becker.

Tennis players are always looking for a winning edge, and on paper, if it's affordable (big if), hiring a coach makes eminent sense. But there's almost always some fly in the ointment. Take the case of a top player (I won't say his name) I talked to a couple of years ago, post Andre and pre-Andy. His agent initially called me, and I talked with the agent a couple of times. Then the agent said, "You really need to speak to _____."

So I spoke to him. The conversation lasted around one minute. It turned out the whole thing had been the agent's idea. The player just said, "I'm happy with the way things are."

"OK," I said. (I'm a coach, not a salesman.)

"Man, you'd be too hard for me," the player said.

"You don't even know me," I said.

"I'm happy," he said.

"You're really happy?" I said. This guy had a ton of talent, but was underachieving like crazy.

"Yeah, I'm happy," the player said. "I don't want to be number 1."

Whoa, I thought. *The truth at last.* At that point there was really nothing else to say. (Now the guy is just traveling with his buddy, wasting his talent. So he'll get his wish: He'll never be number 1.)

As this underachieving player correctly sensed, traveling with a coach is an intense thing. First of all, there's the assumption—the demand, even—that this relationship is going to take you somewhere; is going to raise your game significantly. That's a lot of pressure on both parties.

But just as intense is the psychological aspect. There you are, two guys traveling in very close proximity. Eating meals together, hitting tennis balls together. Spending almost every waking hour together. There's a very high probability that sooner or later—and most likely sooner— one of you is going to start to annoy the other. It's an innately strange relationship that has to be pitched just right if it's going to work out. Some guys like to leave the relationship at the courts: They want space. Other guys don't. The coach works for the player but has to be able to demand a lot from the player, and demand it fearlessly. Likewise, the player will (and must) demand a lot from the coach, who must provide it selflessly.

It's extremely easy for things to go wrong—and I can name you any number of examples where they have.

There has to be a deep compatibility to start with between the two of you, covering many things both spoken and unconscious. In other words: The vibe has to be exactly right. I've turned down any number of potential jobs (and a load of money) because that vibe wasn't there. With Andre and Andy, as you've gathered if you've read this far, the vibe was there in spades. (A shared sense of humor is a total prerequisite.)

It's a lot like a marriage, with a couple of obvious

differences. One of the biggest of which is this: Both of you know, going in, that one of you—or with any luck, both of you mutually—will end this working relationship someday. I never worry about getting fired. I don't like to second-guess myself, and I don't like to think about the way other people coach. The way I see it, I'm me, quirks and all, but it takes two to tango. And if things don't work out, it's not going to be fun, but so be it.

But with any real luck, that person who continues to mean so much to you will always be just a phone call and a smile away.

I realize I've talked a whole lot about the part of coaching that goes on before and after tennis matches, and not nearly as much about what happens *during*.

This is mainly because tennis—unlike football; baseball; basketball; boxing; soccer; cricket; and, for all I know, horseshoes—has this wacky rule that says you *can't* coach during a match. Exactly why this is, I'm not sure. I certainly don't agree with it. The difference between me and some other tennis coaches is that I also don't do it. I have no repertoire of third-base-coach signals. As in (hypothetically, of course): Finger on the right side of the nose means: Serve wide. On the left side: Serve down the middle. Scratching the ear: Work the forehand. Et cetera. Hypothetically.

I could never do it. I'm just too conspicuous—the terrible price of success. (I'm joking.)

Yet I'm also part serious. I really do disagree with the no-coaching rule, and changing it would be one of the only improvements I would ever suggest for tennis. When people talk about going back to wooden racquets, decreasing the size of the service box, et cetera, I tell them they're just annoying me. The way I feel about tennis is, it's stood the test of time. And I think the game is getting better every year.

But the no-coaching rule is the most disappointing part of my job. There's so much going on in my head during every match, so much I can't say—it makes me nuts! If only there were one time-out per set, or even per match, I think major matches would be so much deeper and more interesting. Take Andy's semifinal loss to Tim Henman at last year's Paris Indoor. It wasn't a Grand Slam, but it was still a big match. And it was a killer for Andy. Henman won it in two tiebreakers, taking the first breaker 7–4 and the second, 9–7.

I really do feel I failed Andy that day. (We, not he, really lost that match. Or maybe it was just me.) I don't think I told him enough beforehand about how certain facets of his game matched up against Tim's. And that realization sank in deeper and deeper as the match progressed: I was dying a thousand deaths out there. If only I could've talked to Andy after the first set of that match. . . . If only.

I would have had a million things to say. But if we're imagining a theoretical time-out rule, I guess we also have to imagine a time limit (say twenty seconds), so here are two things I really wish I'd told him: *Listen,* I would have said. *You've got a wicked kick on your second serve—I'd really like you to try and come to net on it now and then. I think it would throw him off, put him on the defensive.* And also: *Every time you're serving your second serve in the deuce court, you've got to work his forehand; he's killing you with the chip-and-charge when you serve down the middle.*

Just those two ideas might have made the tiny bit of difference that could have swung that match the other way. Hey, Andy might've lost anyway (Henman was red hot that week, having also beaten Guga Kuerten and Roger Federer, and he went on to win the tournament) but I would've felt I'd helped him more. Plus, it would have introduced a whole other level of strategy (not to mention competition), since Henman's coach Paul Annacone undoubtedly would've had a thing or two to tell Tim in our imaginary twenty-second NBA-style time-out. I have great respect for Paul—he's done terrific things for Henman, and also had an amazing run with Pete Sampras. There are a number of guys traveling with coaches these days, and I believe some of those coaches aren't as good as they think they are. Maybe a change in the coaching rule would call a few bluffs!

For now, though, the rule remains unchanged.

And so, if you've seen me on TV at one tournament or another, sitting in the stands and staring out like a sunglasses-wearing statue, you might have wondered: *What's he doing there?* "There's Andy's coach, Brad Gilbert," the commentators always say. That's about all they *can* say. With that poker face I wear on the sidelines, I'm not giving them much to work with.

In fact, though, what I'm doing is giving Andy as much to work with as the rules allow.

Andy's previous coach was French. He was emotional. He lived and died on every point. And it made Andy a little uncomfortable.

When you see me on television, I'm wearing black and looking calm. It may not look like I'm doing anything but watching a tennis match. Look again.

In fact, I'm working hard. My job is to convey mental strength and solidity to Andy with the absolute minimum of movement. Andre was different. With Andre, most of the job happened before the match. He'd been on the tour for eight years before we went to work together. He was independent, and his brain was wired differently from Andy's. Andre wanted me there, of course, but it didn't matter if I glanced down or sideways now and then.

Andy, though, likes to look at me for confirmation after every point, whether he wins the point or not, and he wants me to be *there*. Looking strong and sure.

I need to be totally focused on every point. Andy doesn't like me to banter with anyone near me; he doesn't even like me to look right or left. (I always try to sit in the end seats so my head doesn't do that back-and-forth tennis-match thing. That's for me as much as for him: I hate looking side to side.)

And I need to be totally focused on the changeover, because Andy's looking to me then, too. I might just give the smallest fist-pump then, very subtle, meaning (if he's behind), *Come on, just push through it*, or (if he's ahead), *Yes.*

Does it sound like Andy's being demanding? Of course he is—he has every right to be. Because I made him a promise: *No matter what, I've got your back. Whatever it is. And when you go into battle, I'm there.*

Something I love doing—I began with Andre and continue with Andy—is handicapping tennis matches. The best kind is a round of 16 or quarterfinal on our side of the draw of a big tournament, with two tough competitors, where the winner is going to play my guy. "Who do you think is going to win this one?" I'll say, casually. And then my guy will give his opinion, and then I'll say, "Really—what makes you think so?"

Andre was amazing at this. People used to say he was aloof about tennis—I can't even tell you how wrong that is. He's not only incredibly insightful about any given matchup, about what it's going to take for a given player to win on a given day, but passionate about expressing his opinions. As much of a genius off the court as he is on. I call him The Surgeon.

And Andy may have only been at this for a few years, but he has a great head for the game, too. (And he's never shy about expressing an opinion on any subject.) The first time I threw my handicapping hook out, he went right for it, instinctively recognizing that, even if the match is on the other side of the draw, it's a cool exercise.

For one thing, putting his mind on other people is a good way of defusing his prematch nerves. For another, it's a great way for me to learn more about what goes on inside his head. I know the game pretty well, I have thirty years of perspective, and I always have a ton of ideas about any given tennis situation—and the best way for me to go stale would be to think that I know it all. Plus, it's easy for me to get too intense about my own match.

What's more (I always try to remember this), *I'm not the one out there*. As much as I know, Andy's the guy who's got to walk out onto that court. I'm not the one who's faced Philippoussis's serve. And here's the bonus: Once Andy starts to tell me X, Y, and Z about that serve, he's subliminally preparing for the next time he plays Philippoussis.

Subliminal coaching, preparation without pressure—just what the doctor ordered.

One of the first times Andy and I tried it out was during a little event called the U.S. Open, last year at Flushing Meadow. No pressure there!

Andy had had a blazing summer, with three hard-court titles in July and August, at Indianapolis, Montreal, and Cincinnati. Suddenly he couldn't walk three steps without someone shoving a microphone in his face and asking if he was the Future of American Tennis. No pressure! All eyes were on him at the Open, and I had to not only prepare him for each match, but to keep him—and myself—on an even keel. To keep things light.

So during the quarterfinals, I dangled a little hook. Who did he like, I asked, in the Federer-Nalbandian match?

All of a sudden, the Future of American Tennis was no longer an issue. Andy smiled a little—I could practically see the wheels turning as he thought about it. He told me that even though Federer was coming off his win at Wimbledon and was seeded second here, he, Andy, liked Nalbandian, and he told me why: Nalbandian had dominated Federer both in the juniors and so far on the pro tour. Nalbandian's power groundstroke game matched up well against Federer's touch, and even though Federer had momentum on the tour in general, Nalbandian had momentum in the rivalry.

He turned out to be exactly right. Nalbandian won in four sets.

But unwittingly (or maybe only partly wittingly) Andy

had done some good mental preparation for his match after next—his semifinal against David Nalbandian.

Andy had played Nalbandian twice before, and had killed him both times. But this was the Open, huge stakes, and Nalbandian was having an incredible tournament. And in the other semifinal, played earlier in the day, Andre had lost to Juan Carlos Ferrero, who was also having a hell of a tournament.

So when Andy and Nalbandian walked out into Arthur Ashe Stadium, the buzz of a possible Andre-Andy final was gone, and the crowd was dead. And—remember I told you how the best players are always making adjustments? Nalbandian had thought hard about the last time Andy had killed him, and he'd made adjustments. From the moment the match began, he was ten times the player he'd been before.

And Andy was flat. Between the dead crowd and his own nerves, he played conservatively—not to lose—and very quickly got sucked into playing Nalbandian's match. He had some chances to crack the ball, and he didn't, and Nalbandian ended up moving him left to right and not making mistakes, and then Andy wound up taking risks in some low-percentage situations. Going for the winner when it wasn't there.

First two sets to Nalbandian, 7–6, 6–3.

On the changeover after the second set, I pumped my fist to Andy: *Just push on through.*

Up to now, it had been a very uneventful match: Nalbandian was just missing nothing. The crowd stayed asleep. But then in the third, a seemingly small thing happened that turned the tide. Andy was serving at 3–3, and fell behind, 15–40. Yet somehow he was able to gut out the game—and just like that, Nalbandian was the one who was playing not to lose.

As strong as he was, he had had an epic, three hour and forty-five minute battle the day before against Morocco's Younes El-Aynaoui, and he only had so much gas left in the tank. Deep down, Nalbandian knew that if he couldn't shut down Andy in the third, he wouldn't have anything left for the fourth.

Which is exactly what happened. Facing match point in the third-set tiebreaker, Andy unleashed a 138-mile-an-hour bomb to the backhand that buckled Nalbandian's racquet and broke his will. He then cruised home, 6–1, 6–3. It was a very big moment: For the first time in our time together—and in the biggest tournament of his life—he had survived a lackluster start to gut out a brutal five-setter.

I was elated. I was beyond elated. I thought of what I once told Andre: *This is what everything is about. If you can win a match playing at 60 percent of where you feel your game really is, but you're 100 percent mentally, that's way better than if you're hitting the ball like a dream, but you're only 60 percent there mentally.* I knew that this was exactly the kind of tough match a player had to learn to win in order to get through to (possibly) easier matches later on.

And now I knew Andy Roddick could win the U.S. Open. But I summoned up all my willpower and remembered Chiv. I kept my game face on. No celebrating. K.I.T.

Andy was tired and sore after that match. He had a long rub, and then we got ATP trainer Doug Spreen (who now works with Andy full time) to come over to the hotel in Manhattan to treat some very bad blisters on the balls of his feet. Andy was starving, but he was too tired to go to a restaurant, so I went up to one of my five favorite restaurants ever, Campagnola, on the Upper East Side, where Frankie D., who runs the show, knows just what we like. Andy powered up with a big order: tomato and mozzarella, Caesar salad, chicken parmesan, gnocchi with pesto. Vittles the Night Before. Time to relax, talk a little about tennis, a lot about other things. There was football on TV that night, and so we watched the game while we ate. Then Andy got a good night's sleep.

We'd said next to nothing about tomorrow.

On final day, we went out to Flushing Meadow around noon, and warmed up from one to one twenty-five on Practice Court 5—right next to Ferrero! Andy had to get his blisters taped even for practice. He was still pretty sore. We were just trying to get his body to a point where it would be in pretty good shape by 4:00 P.M. There was no chance he would feel perfect; I just wanted to get him feeling better. (Fortunately, Ferrero's four-setter against Andre the day before probably hadn't left him feeling fresh as a daisy, either.)

At the end of practice, we did what has become a ritual: I feed Andy six to ten balls that he whacks, baseball-style, with the handle end of the racquet. And let me tell you, he can take some pretty good cuts—he hit a few of those balls halfway to Shea Stadium.

Afterward, we relaxed in the training room while Andy had his tape removed and iced his arm. Then we went up to the players' lounge for lunch. We watched a little more football on the big-screen TV in the lounge while Andy indulged in one of his favorite pastimes—busting my chops about my beloved Oakland Raiders. (At that point, in late August, I was still excited about the Raiders' upcoming season. Little did I know that it would turn into a 4–12 debacle.)

Andy had a lot of K.I.T. in his game that day. At about 3:30, we went down to the locker room to wait for the match. The final was supposed to start at 4:00, but between the televised football and the prematch ceremony, the start kept getting delayed—it wound up turning into almost a half hour. It didn't matter to Andy: He was relaxed and funny, on top of his (nontennis) game. At that point we were still in the midst of our "back in the day" ban. So as we sat there in the locker room, he tried to snooker me. "So, Brad—tell me about your first Open," Andy said.

I gave him a look. "Nice try," I told him.

It was the calm before the storm. There was no discussion at all of what was about to take place.

Then the word came in: Five minutes till go-time.

Andy looked around to make sure he had everything in his bag, stood up. Then, and only then, did I talk to him about the match. It was the opposite of the big game day speech. The opposite of, "Jeez, here we are in the finals of the U.S. Open." Andy knew where he was. All too well.

I wanted to focus him on the task at hand. I wanted to let him know where I thought his advantages were. I wanted to convey to Andy that this was, before anything else, a tennis match—just another match. "Use your forehand," I told him. "The guy doesn't have a great return— he returns a lot right at you. I think you might be able to serve-and-volley a little bit today."

Then I gave his fist a pound with mine, slapped him on the back, and told him the truest thing I could think of about this moment: "You're forty pounds heavier than he is. You're bigger; you're stronger. Go and impose your will on him."

Andy smiled a little. Then he walked out onto the court.

No matter what, I've got your back.
Whatever it is. And when you go into battle, I'm there.